Inspiring minds and imaginations since 1910

Gordon School
Inspiring minds and imaginations since 1910

Published by:
Gordon School
45 Maxfield Avenue
East Providence, Rhode Island 02914

ISBN: 978-0-9762831-2-6

Editorial Committee:
Michael Hamilton, Noah Davis '97, Ralph Wales, Kerri Hayes, Kerrie Donahue, Siobhan Welsh, Geoff Griffin, Cindy Elder

Photo Credits:
Geoff Griffin, Options Photography, Mary Beth Meehan, David Silverman, and many other photographers through the decades who have helped to capture the Gordon story.

Special thanks to Kim Ridley, Maryanne Pieri, Maureen Kelly, Danny Karpf, Lynn Bowman, Emily Anderson, Paola Martinez and many other members of the Gordon faculty who helped during the editorial process.

Copyright © Gordon School
All rights reserved.

No part of this publication may be reproduced, stored in a retrieval system,
or transmitted, in any form or by any means—electronic, mechanical,
photocopying, recording, or otherwise, without prior written permission from the publisher.

Printed in the United States of America by The Kutztown Publishing Co., Inc.
Kutztown, Pennsylvania 19530

Printed on recycled paper.

CONTENTS

Introduction
5

History
6

Spaces
18

Learning
36

Community
98

This book is dedicated to Dr. Helen West Cooke, whose vision for educating the whole child led to the creation of the Gordon School in 1910. Dr. Cooke's belief that children should be respected as individuals and encouraged to engage in "the true spirit of joyous work" has graduated thousands of students who have gone on to make a profound difference in the world around them.

Introduction

"I believe in studying into the individual character of each child and seeing how each one should be trained."

These words of Gordon's founder Dr. Helen West Cooke, contained in a journal entry entitled modestly "Ideas on the Bringing Up of Children," pulse with vitality as Gordon celebrates its centennial.

Dr. Cooke's ideas revealed her wisdom as a practicing pediatrician (a rare choice for a woman at the time) and, even more basically, the instinct of a mother. Dr. Cooke's decision to start her own school came from her dissatisfaction with her oldest son's education. When her second son Gordon turned six, Dr. Cooke took matters into her own hands, turning her living room into a classroom. And so the story began.

In that first year, Gordon Cooke and his classmate, Margaret Arthur, learned actively. How could it have been otherwise? They had Dr. Cooke's close attention and the stimulus of New England's crisp autumn air. Among Cooke's ideas was the belief that fresh air – carried through open windows year round – promoted sharp thinking and good health.

Today at Gordon, we proudly carry Dr. Cooke's ideas, instincts and entrepreneurial spirit into the twenty-first century. Led by her example, we appreciate that excellence in the schoolhouse rests on a sound, three-way partnership: a commitment shared by a teacher, a child's parents and a child.

We believe each child comes to school with boundless curiosity, the need to be understood fully and the inclination, unless taught differently, to see the world with hope and optimism. We expect the adults to bring intellect, empathy and an unwavering commitment to the hard and vital work ahead.

There's no single recipe, only the conscious cultivation and sustenance of this human foundation of school, home and child. It is within this context that children's unique characteristics – both their strengths and their vulnerabilities – are made evident.

This book highlights the continuous work, the focus and the commitment behind educational excellence: a tale of gritty engagement, a child-by-child approach that defies any unilateral formula.

We see our school's basic worth in the grainy black and white photographs from our beginnings and in the more recent collages of colored portraits of learning that fill these pages. We know that you will, too. Turn a page and witness a mother's dream fulfilled: boys and girls engaged in what Dr. Cooke called "the true spirit of joyous work."

Ralph L. Wales, Head of School, September 2010

History
1910-1929

Teach our boys and girls together, and in the "Open-Air". Awaken interest and stimulate investigation. Develop the individuality of the child by encouraging free self-expression. Instill the true spirit of joyous work.
– from the 1915 prospectus of Dr. Helen West Cooke's "Open-Air School," which would be renamed the Gordon School

Dr. Cooke listens as her students read. (l-r) Margaret Arthur, Gordon Cooke and Edith Peckham formed the first class in 1910.

Dr. Helen West Cooke set a humble goal when she embarked upon the path that would lead to the creation of the Gordon School. She wanted to establish a learning environment for her six-year-old son, Gordon, where he would feel respected, nurtured and encouraged to ask questions.

Born on February 11, 1873, Dr. Cooke attended Rhode Island elementary schools during an era when strict discipline and corporal punishment were the norm. Her philosophy of education grew in part from these experiences. She knew education could, and should, be different.

"I believe in treating children as you would dear friends, asking them to do things, not telling them," Dr. Cooke wrote in her journal during the years she worked as one of New England's few female physicians. Her medical practice also led her to a firm belief in the value of fresh air, a simple but effective way to keep young minds alert and young bodies healthy.

And so, during the fall of 1910, Gordon Cooke and his playmate, Margaret Arthur, sat at two desks in the converted nursery of the Cooke's home at 405 Angell Street on the East Side of Providence, while the boy's mother taught the pair. She kept the windows of the room open throughout the year, a practice which lent Rhode Island's only coeducational, independent elementary school its original name: "The Open-Air School."

By the end of the year, a third pupil – Edith Peckham – had joined Gordon and Margaret. In the fall of 1911, the trio grew to ten students, and two new instructors signed on: French teacher F. Ellis Jackson and music teacher Lenora Bennett. In developing her early curriculum, Dr. Cooke drew on the philosophy of John Dewey, who believed that children learn by doing and by relating new ideas to what they already know.

As word spread about this novel approach to education, more families expressed interest in participating. Increasing enrollment drew mild concern from Dr. Cooke's mother, who worried for her health. "Although I do not propose to start a school, I think I might manage a few more," Dr. Cooke assured her mother. Little could she imagine that, one hundred years later, her school would serve more than four hundred students each year and be known across the nation for innovations in education and multicultural teaching.

By September 1914, eighty students called "The Open-Air School" their educational home. More pupils meant more classrooms. The school built two new rooms and transformed the attic into teaching space. To keep the family feeling alive at the growing school, Dr. Cooke expanded room by room, rather than by erecting a single large structure. Her keen understanding of the impact of physical environment on students would become a firm principle in the school's architectural design through years of remodeling and expansion, an awareness which continues to this day.

Early photographs reveal students actively involved in their learning. Dramatic productions, student newspapers and compilations of poetry and fiction showcased the students' accomplishments. Everywhere, there was evidence of the faculty's efforts to foster confident learners whose work was honored and respected. Equally evident was the high degree of parental involvement in the school – not surprising, given the school's beginnings in a parent's home.

In 1917, Gordon and eight other sixth graders proudly became the school's first graduating class. That same year, the founder wrote that she strove to "instill the true spirit of joyous work" in her charges, a core tenet that remains at the heart of the institution's philosophy one hundred years later.

Seeing the need for an educational experience to take students through secondary school, Dr. Cooke and a committee of eight parents helped to found Providence Country Day School in 1923. With this development, boys graduated from Dr. Cooke's school after fifth grade, often continuing on to Providence Country Day, while girls remained until seventh grade. Today, the school's individualized secondary school placement program echoes the same concern Dr. Cooke had for students seeking to further their growth after their years at Gordon.

Over the next few decades, the school would experiment with various grade levels, eventually deciding on a nursery through eighth grade configuration which encouraged young children to blossom in a secure environment, while enabling young adults to take on a leadership role within their school community.

The 1920s were a time of expansion. The school's first gymnasium was built in 1923; the library came along a year later. The enduring tradition of assemblies started in 1926 with representatives from all grades reporting their classes' success to fellow students, much as they do today in "town meetings," assemblies and presentations which help students build confidence in public speaking. In 1927, the school relocated the fourth and fifth grade to the recently purchased Wallace House on Angell Street.

As the 1920s roared to a close, the institution continued to carve out its special place in the Rhode Island landscape. The school which Dr. Cooke had created to educate her son was incorporated in the last year of the decade as "The Gordon School."

The sixth grade, Class of 1920, poses outside the upper grade classroom, formerly Dr. Cooke's photography studio.

GORDON SCHOOL

1930-1949

Working and playing; achieving and sharing; helping and being helped; expressing and keeping silence; projecting and pausing; conforming and creating – these have given rhythm to our year. It has been a joyous rhythm.
— Margaret Fulton Coe, Headmistress, 1935-36

Field Day had become a time-honored tradition at Gordon when this photo was taken in the late 1930s. This day of friendly competition remains a high point for students today.

The early 1930s found the Gordon School at a critical crossroads, and the next decade would help to define its future. On February 24, 1931, Dr. Cooke resigned as Headmistress due to the failing health of her husband, Dr. Henry Cooke. She remained on the Board of Trustees, dividing her time between Providence and their home in Peterborough, New Hampshire for many years. The school began the challenging task of choosing a suitable replacement. The school's Executive Committee scoured the country and selected Katherine Rusk, a lifelong educator who was serving as the Principal of Waynflete Latin School in Portland, Maine.

Simultaneously, the Great Depression enveloped the country. Students were aware of events unfolding around them – "We, of the Gordon School, with our comfortable homes, good food and luxuries, have indeed much to be grateful for," read an eighth grade editorial in 1931.

Teachers, administrators and parents saw to it that the educational institution remained a sanctuary during these difficult times. "Education is concerned with the whole child, recognizing him as a physical, emotional, mental and spiritual being," read a catalogue from the early 1930s.

Despite the financial struggles of the country, Gordon teachers continued to nurture all aspects of young students. In addition to traditional subjects, physical education remained a focus. The campus sported four playgrounds and two play platforms. The upper school was divided into the Greens and the Grays, who competed throughout the year for the school banner. A newly formed Gordon Parents Association helped coordinate lectures, activities and field trips, and the student government met for the first time in 1932.

However, the country's woeful economic condition affected the school behind the scenes. Although Dr. Cooke reported her "great pride and satisfaction" in Gordon at its 25th anniversary celebration in 1935, enrollment had dropped to 115 students from a high of 160 four years prior. Furthermore, Rusk fell ill before the start of the school year, and Margaret Fulton Coe, her former colleague at Baltimore's Park School, took over as Acting Headmistress until the end of the year.

When Sarah Hincks, Principal of the Shady Hill Country Day School in Chestnut Hill, Pennsylvania, joined as Headmistress in the summer of 1936, the enrollment and financial picture had become increasingly dire. With just 107 students enrolled, the administration cut costs where possible, while maintaining curriculum standards and teacher salaries.

As the Board persevered through these challenges, teachers continued to encourage their charges to "learn by doing." In 1936, the third grade created their own Norse society in a classroom converted into a Viking hall. The project interwove music, art, history, mathematics and political debate in a program which completely immersed students in a culture very different from their own. Decades later, this type of experiential learning would become a formal part of the fifth grade curriculum known as "immersion week," when students recreate elements of an ancient culture in their classroom.

With finances continuing to sag, in March 1938, the Board announced that Providence Country Day would assume management of Gordon. Edward Lund, PCD's headmaster (whose four children attended Gordon), appointed Margaret "Poggy" Langdon as the school's Director, replacing the departing Sarah Hincks.

Langdon moved her family to Dr. Cooke's old quarters and set about reviving the beloved institution. She reached further into the community, courting students from a wider range of ethnic and geographic backgrounds. Langdon made it clear that anti-semitism would not be condoned at Gordon, and slowly but surely, her actions planted the seeds for the school's inclusive culture.

Parents were increasingly involved, as Langdon believed that "the close cooperation of the parents is an important factor in making Gordon meaningful." The school held square dances for the parents in the gym, proving that physical activity wasn't just for students. White replaced gray as one of the school colors, and art teacher Dorothy Greenough designed a new silhouette logo.

As World War II raged in Europe, enrollment trended upward. A 1943 photo essay in the *The Providence Sunday Journal* depicted Gordon students engaged in knitting, making lap boards for hospitalized soldiers and sailors, and buying war stamps. "Gordon School children, from the ten-year-olds down to the smallest nursery pupils, are making their contribution to the war effort," the article noted. "The activities are scaled down so that each one, however small, may participate in the program."

In March 1944, months after giving birth to her third daughter, Langdon announced her resignation. With the approval of Providence Country Day, a governing board elected by the newly revitalized Gordon Parents' Association installed Florence Robinson, Lower School Head at the Ogontz School in Pennsylvania, as the new Headmistress. By 1945, enrollment reached 136. Two years later, the school announced the end of the legal and financial relationship with Providence Country Day. The school had successfully endured a challenging period in history, emerging stronger from the process.

Poggy Langdon, Director of School, 1938-1944.

1950-1969

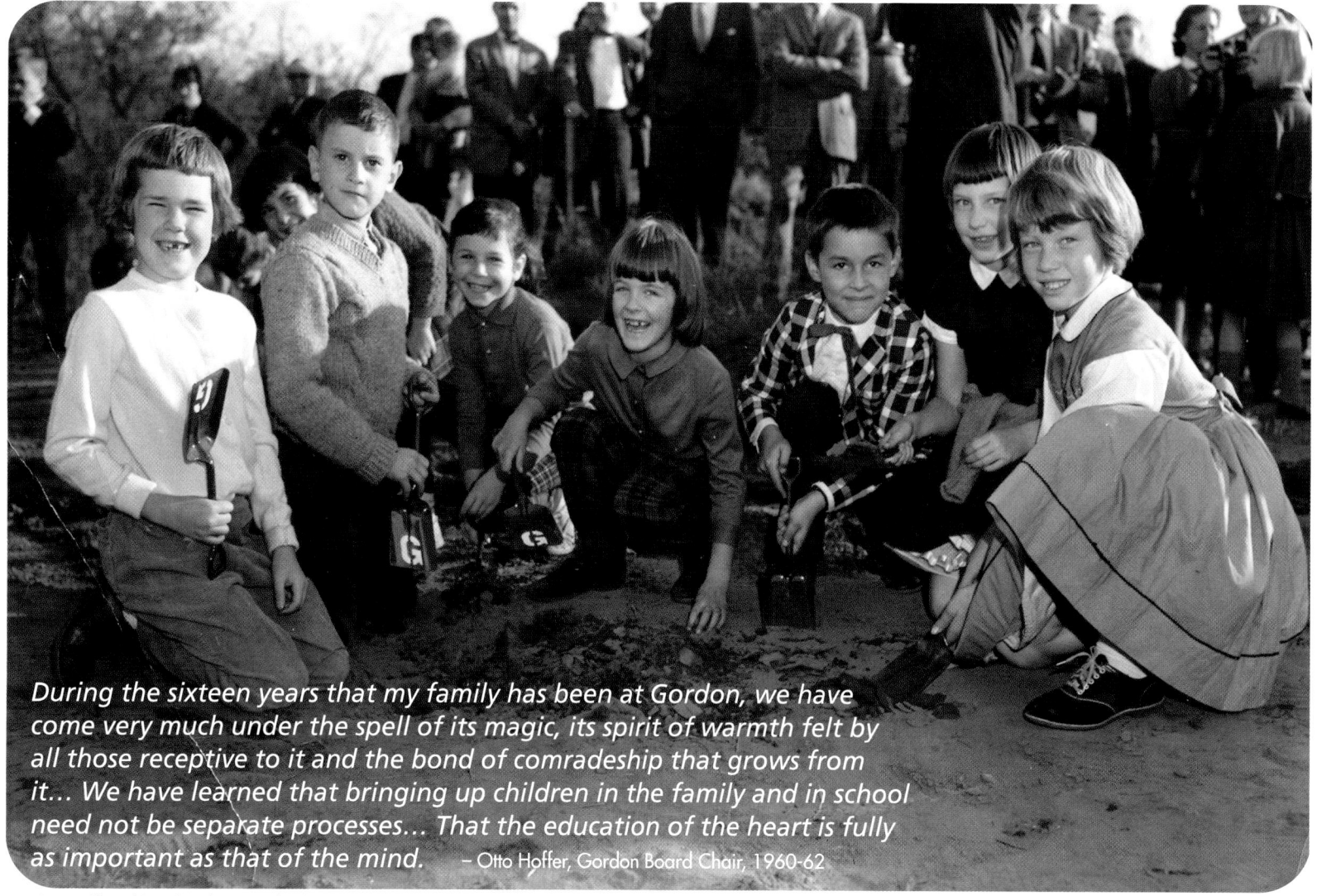

During the sixteen years that my family has been at Gordon, we have come very much under the spell of its magic, its spirit of warmth felt by all those receptive to it and the bond of comradeship that grows from it... We have learned that bringing up children in the family and in school need not be separate processes... That the education of the heart is fully as important as that of the mind. – Otto Hoffer, Gordon Board Chair, 1960-62

Groundbreaking for the new facility in East Providence on Sunday, October 29, 1961. Taking part were second graders (l-r) Peggy Stoll, (unidentified), Monique Scheuer, Jane Thomas, Jay Aldrich, Kate Miller and Julie Blount.

The Gordon School celebrated its fortieth anniversary in 1950. Dr. Cooke officially resigned from the Board, but returned immediately as an honorary lifetime member. That same year, the institution broke the color barrier, welcoming its first African-American student. While two families removed their children because of this step, many more cited the school's inclusiveness as a reason for educating their children at Gordon. In a move foreshadowing the school's later commitment to diversity, the Board voted for a policy of considering applications of any child regardless of race, color or religion.

Florence Robinson, who successfully piloted the school after the end of its affiliation with Providence Country Day, announced her retirement in February 1956. Gordon's Board found a replacement in Frederic Locke, a twenty-nine-year-old Yale graduate who was teaching sixth grade at New Canaan Country School.

During Locke's tenure, the first carnival delighted students with a fathers' midway and a mothers' market in the spring of 1957. The event raised $2,100 and was deemed a "brilliant success." The next fall, parents organized the inaugural book fair. Both traditions, overseen by parent committees, continue to the present day.

By the beginning of the 1958-59 school year, enrollment had reached a high of 173 students, but the physical plant struggled to meet the needs of this growing population. Gordon's Board recruited two respected educators, Paulina Olsen, Lower School Head at New Caanan Country School, and Edward Yeomans, Headmaster at Shady Hill School, to assess the school and grounds and make suggestions for improvement. In a report which would profoundly impact the future of the school, the pair specifically noted the success of Gordon's child-centered education. "I have seldom seen such a healthy or happy group of children, or a group that was so obviously respected and appreciated by the teachers," Olsen wrote. Their ultimate conclusion, however, was simple but firm: "The school plant has outlived its usefulness. The school should move."

As the Board considered this verdict, it also had to replace Locke, who moved to a school in Colorado. They hired Laurance P. "Larry" Miller, Assistant Headmaster at Hackley School in Tarrytown, New York. By the time he retired twenty years later, Miller had made an enduring mark on Gordon, increasing the school's enrollment through the 1960s, overseeing the move to a new campus, and setting the school on a clear path toward the future.

Miller's first task was to find a new location. After considering space on the East Side, the Board chose a seven-and-a-half acre plot on Maxfield Avenue in East Providence. The site was identified by Board Chair Otto Hoffer, who discovered it during one of his frequent walks on a wooded piece of property where he enjoyed hunting for mushrooms.

In September 1961, Gordon's Board, led by Buildings and Grounds Chair Dr. Eugene M. Nelson, chose William Warner, an accomplished architect, to take on his first school project. Simultaneously, they launched a $250,000 fundraising drive. A month later, more than one hundred students excitedly used play shovels to break ground for the Warner design.

Although teachers and students expected to begin the 1962-63 school year in the new space, construction slowed and 405 Angell Street opened one last time. During winter break, parents and students helped move supplies, books and classroom furniture from Angell Street to Maxfield Avenue. The caravan of vehicles and the enthusiasm of parent and student volunteers showed that the true Gordon spirit of pitching in and learning by doing reached far beyond the classroom walls.

The building design, which paid homage to the Angell Street campus by separating sections of the school, won the childrens' hearts. Warner had wisely consulted students, along with faculty, parents and administrators, before drawing his plans. As a result, the unique architectural structures incorporated the perspectives of the community's youngest members. The three-quarter scale featured low ceilings in the halls, while pyramid-shaped roofs in classrooms reached upward to fourteen feet. The translucent panels at the top allowed light into the learning spaces, and all classrooms had a door to the outdoors, reflecting Gordon's original "open air" policy.

For many children, their first exposure to Gordon came in the form of summer camp, started in 1965 under the direction of Florence McKenna with help from Gordon teacher Ruth Winn. The school's beautiful setting created the perfect backdrop for activities in crafts, music, nature, science, athletics, games and storytelling.

Across the nation, the 1960s saw schools rethinking strategies and trying out new concepts, both in curriculum and organization of space. Gordon was no exception. In 1965, Miller proposed dramatic changes designed to increase enrollment from 200 to 350 and reduce the risk that Gordon would become overly exclusive. His new plan called for double sections for nursery through eighth grade, reducing class size to eighteen students. A Middle School division would be formed of the upper four grades and housed in a new building. Furthermore, the Middle School would create large, open classrooms including students grouped by division rather than by grade. Parents enthusiastically endorsed the proposal.

Gordon tapped Warner again, asking him to build a Middle School building and gymnasium. Construction, set to be complete by September of 1969, was delayed by a carpenters' strike, and eighty middle schoolers started the year in Hope Congregational Church on the Wampanoag Trail. Miller made daily trips to the temporary campus, ensuring that all of the school's 304 students felt safe and at home in both new locations.

Larry Miller, Headmaster, 1959-1980.

GORDON SCHOOL

1970-1989

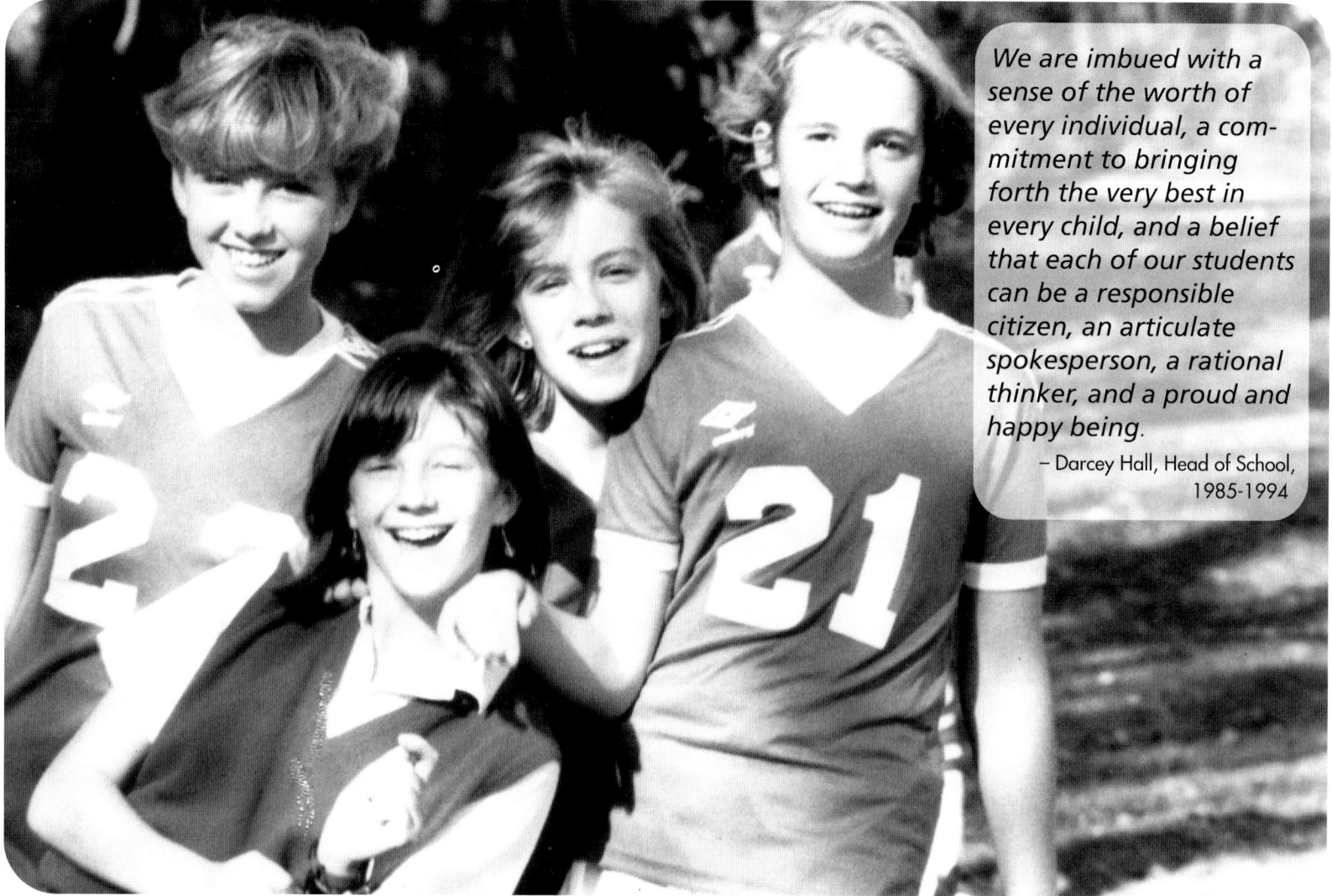

> *We are imbued with a sense of the worth of every individual, a commitment to bringing forth the very best in every child, and a belief that each of our students can be a responsible citizen, an articulate spokesperson, a rational thinker, and a proud and happy being.*
> – Darcey Hall, Head of School, 1985-1994

From the playing field to the classroom, Gordon students learn to play and work as a team.

The 1970s dawned with the Lower and Middle Schools reunited at 45 Maxfield Avenue. The new Middle School building included four teaching lofts, a science lab, art studios and a workshop. Designed by Warner, it featured the trademark architecture of the existing buildings, scaled up to accommodate the older students whose footsteps echoed through the halls. Here, young adults gained a space uniquely their own, a building which reflected their own growth and development.

The sports program expanded to include gymnastics, volleyball and basketball, in addition to the soccer teams already established.

Up until this time, a Gordon education had been available primarily to those with the financial means to afford full tuition. The 1970s saw an emerging awareness of the need to create endowed funds to provide financial aid to students who would otherwise be unable to attend. The Albanese Fund was the first of many such endowments which would begin to open the doors of the Gordon School to a wider community. Likewise, grateful parents and alumni increasingly left their mark on the school by creating endowed funds dedicated to financial aid, general operations and academic programs.

Larry Miller announced his retirement in 1980. A study conducted with parents that year reached conclusions which would have made Dr. Cooke proud: "The Gordon School is a community of students, parents and teachers where the focus of education is on the individual development of each child." Her philosophy had remained at the core of the school for seventy years.

In 1981, the "gator" became the school's sports mascot, an enduring symbol of school pride, chosen by students for its Gordon green.

Eugene Ruth, Jr. replaced Miller and quickly moved to end the open classroom system of the last decade, reflecting a general trend in education. Enrollment began to climb, and Ruth hired the school's first business manager, Bradford Johnson, a Gordon parent. As a result of costly building projects and falling enrollment numbers, they discovered Gordon had been running at a deficit for five years. The Board launched a $500,000 capital campaign, a goal that was reached in February 1983. A month later, Ruth stepped down and Thomas Fulton became interim headmaster. He remained for two years, helping Gordon through a period of transition.

On the world stage in 1983, Gordon received recognition for its commitment to helping others. In October of that year, the nationally televised show *20/20* highlighted Gordon's focus on community service. The program featured Gordon students who had raised $375 by raking leaves, babysitting and running errands, and had used those funds to sponsor Heera Mainya Niraula, a seven-year-old Nepalese girl, through the "Save the Children" fund. The television crew visited Heera deep in the Himalayas and brought the story full circle for Gordon students, who stared wide-eyed at televised images of a young Nepalese girl who now felt more like a friend.

In 1984, the Gordon Parents Association donated four computers, and the school established its first computer lab. Gordon would continue to keep pace with the digital explosion by introducing more computers, technology and innovative educational methodology as the computer age unfolded.

At Gordon's seventy-fifth anniversary celebration on May 18, 1985, the Board introduced Dorothy "Darcey" Hall as the new Head of School. The school's leadership laid out a plan to achieve financial stability, increase enrollment and improve Gordon's visibility and image within the community.

Hall prided herself on keeping abreast of everything that occurred under the many pyramid-shaped roofs. She had a boundless work ethic. "Darcey is energy," Pat Emmet, an adored kindergarten teacher, wrote years later on the occasion of the Head's retirement.

One of Hall's priorities was to strengthen Gordon's ties with its original home, the East Side community. She commissioned the school's first history, *The Gordon School Story, 1910-1994* by Mark Dunkelman, a Gordon parent. Hall proved to be a skilled networker with past parents, alumni and newer residents of Providence and surrounding towns.

The school became the first elementary school accepted as a member of the Coalition of Essential Schools, a national educational reform movement led by Theodore Sizer. The Coalition's core principles mirrored Gordon's educational philosophy: integrated curricula, active student-centered instructions and inclusive decision making. "Gordon's strength and special character is its educational program, which recognizes the unique qualities of each child," the Coalition concluded, a characterization which undoubtedly would have delighted Dr. Cooke. Although formal engagement with the Coalition ended in the late 1990s, the values that inspired this partnership remain embedded in the school's work today.

In May 1988, the administration added a service learning element to the eighth grade curriculum developed by Gordon teacher Joann Watson, which remains a meaningful component of the students' experience during their final year at Gordon. To this day, all eighth graders devote several weeks of their graduating year to off-site service projects at one of a variety of social service agencies. The year culminates with presentations by the eighth graders to an audience of faculty, family members and fellow students.

Darcey Hall, Head of School, 1985-1994.

GORDON SCHOOL

1990-2009

Our foremost goal is to instill in each child the love of learning. We facilitate the child's social and emotional growth, stimulate the child's creativity and imagination, develop problem-solving skills and promote work habits that will last a lifetime.
— Maureen Kelly, Early Childhood Director

Members of the Class of 2010 celebrate after a successful science experiment.

Gordon entered the last decade of the millennium on sound educational and financial footing, with enrollment numbers steadily climbing. The Board embarked upon a successful capital campaign in January 1991 to establish endowed funds for faculty salaries and financial aid, as well as facility improvements, including a new fine arts wing.

Darcey Hall resigned as Head of School at the close of the 1993-94 academic year, well-loved by students and parents alike. Gordon chose Ralph L. Wales, Lower School Principal at The Buckley School in Los Angeles, to succeed Hall. He brought with him a passion for multicultural teaching, along with a firm belief in the student-teacher relationship as the key to effective learning.

The school's leadership worked diligently to lay the groundwork for a true multicultural learning environment. During the next decade, representatives from the entire Gordon community engaged in dynamic conversations that produced a detailed strategy to diversify the school's student body and faculty. "In Cooke's vision and in today's practice, Gordon's teachers are guided to apply human measures to their practice," Wales said. "The trust at the foundation of our work requires our daily attention and effort. It is this commitment to the human side of education that allows us all to sleep well at night. With basic trust at the heart of our operation, our children will continue to learn with confidence in ways that endure and transform."

Excellence in teaching continued to bloom in many corners throughout the 1990s, sometimes recognized in formal ways — such as the 1998 Presidential Award for Excellence received by teacher Diana Reeves — but often in much subtler ways, in the form of letters, thank yous and hugs from students and parents who valued their work.

In 1992, the Gordon Community Association established a significant financial aid endowment. The Board, parents and friends of the school raised more than $300,000 through a challenge grant, doubling the school's endowment in 1996. A decade later, the Board made the decision to allocate five percent of all annual fund dollars to the endowment, which continues to grow at a healthy rate. Thanks to what Wales described as "terrifically competent financial management," the institution's endowment exceeded six million dollars in 2010.

With strengthened financial resources, the school embarked on a $6.1 million Campaign for Gordon's Future to improve the school's facilities and expand access to a more diverse population. In 1999, students thrilled to the sight of a big yellow backhoe rolling onto campus to begin the work of building a new two-story library, a new field house with regulation-sized basketball court and comfortable locker rooms, and other improvements which touched every division of the school. Gordon received its largest donation ever in the fall of 2000, an anonymous one-million dollar gift earmarked for the campaign.

"Students arrived in the fall to wonderful new and renovated classrooms in the Sharp Family Early Childhood Center and finished the spring with physical education classes in the state-of-the-art Nelson Field House," recalls Barbara Hendrie, who served as Board Chair during this exciting period. "Whether looking through windows and fences or donning hardhats for an up-close look at the construction underway, students and teachers were able to explore and monitor the progress that was also being made in the Middle and Lower Schools, as well as in what would be a new vibrant hub for the school, the Joukowsky Family Library."

In the midst of this major facility improvement project, the drive for racial diversity continued at a brisk pace. The Board clarified this goal in a 1999 statement: "We believe that student learning is enhanced when a diversity of ideas and perspectives is incorporated into the learning process. When exposed to a variety of viewpoints, students learn to broaden their own perspectives, to think critically, to apply different approaches and to accept a variety of solutions. A diversity of people — those of different races, backgrounds and cultures — is an important source of a diversity of ideas. In providing children with a comprehensive education, we must not only teach them academic skills, but we must also teach the humanistic skills necessary to be successful in a complex and diverse world."

In an effort to further its work in multicultural education, the school hired Jennifer Foley as its first Diversity Director in 2001. The following year, the eighth grade traveled to Alabama to view significant landmarks of the Civil Rights movement and learn about this critical time in American history, a week-long field trip now firmly ingrained in the eighth grade curriculum and permanently funded by endowed sources.

The new Joukowsky Family Library opened in 2001 in typical Gordon fashion, with children, grandparents, mothers, fathers, teachers and staff helping to shelve the 17,000-plus books on brand new shelves. Students in every division made human book chains, passing books hand-to-hand from the old gym, where many of the books were stored, to the new library and into the waiting hands of parent volunteers, who placed them on the shelves.

The year 2001 also brought with it the crushing

Ralph Wales, Head of School, with the Gordon Gator as the school kicked off its Centennial year on Founder's Day, February 11, 2010.

sadness of the September 11th attacks on the World Trade Center and the Pentagon. Once again, Gordon became a sanctuary for its students, while at the same time facing real-world questions within its tight-knit community.

"In the context of the new world that exploded before us on September 11th, age-old questions for educators have new and profound implications," Wales wrote shortly after the attacks. "What is essential and must be taught? What should we teach with our words? What should we teach with our silence? When should we listen to an idea and leave it unchallenged? When must we seize an idea and take a stand?" Questions such as these would fuel courageous decisions and propel the Gordon community closer to its ideals of inclusivity and diversity.

In 2004, the Board passed a plan which enabled the school to assess whether it was creating an environment in which all children could reach their full potential. With the help of educational consultant Enid Lee, Gordon adopted a curriculum in which the discussion of race was encouraged in the classroom. The goal was "to keep race on the table at every level, take the natural curiosity of a child and talk about it," said Wales. Multicultural practice meant teaching all children – not just children of color – with methods and resources that encourage multiple perspectives.

These changes were part of an overall effort to graduate students who would actively participate in the world beyond Gordon. Teachers focused on developing relationships with children that would help them discover the complexity of their identity.

"We need to see that a person's identity is made up of many things," says Kim Ridley, Director of Diversity and Multicultural Practice. "Race, class, gender, ability, sexual orientation and many other things combine to create who we are and how we create a community. Education needs to address how we are going to live together in the future. Sometimes it's hard to see the human being underneath, but that's what we are. We're all just human beings learning to live together."

The institution's groundbreaking work in multicultural education caused independent schools around the country to take note. In 2004, Gordon was recognized as one of the nation's twelve "Leading Edge" schools by the National Association of Independent Schools. The first Rhode Island school to win this award, Gordon was honored for its work in equity and justice.

In 2007, the school hosted its first annual Gordon School Institute on Multicultural Practice, a week-long series of workshops for middle school teaching professionals. Educators from across the United States now consider Gordon a primary resource for learning and discussion of the best multicultural practices.

As Gordon enters its second century, more than 25 percent of the student body and 20 percent of the faculty self-identify as persons of color. The school's facilities are state-of-the-art, the Board and faculty are a driving force of innovation, and the student-centered educational philosophy provides a benchmark for schools everywhere. Not surprisingly, the institution has taken on a new challenge, one which will share the teaching concepts developed at Gordon with a much wider population.

Gordon's centennial year marks the beginning of the Teacher Residency Program at Gordon School and Roger Williams University. Directed by Lynn Bowman, a seasoned Gordon faculty member, this master's program enables graduate students to gain hands-on exposure to multicultural teaching practices, on site at Gordon.

The program is designed to serve educators working in all settings: urban, charter, private and rural schools. Bowman sees it as an opportunity not only for teachers, but for visionary educators and principals who may open the schools of the future.

"Just as it is our intention to send eighth graders out as innovative thinkers who create change in the world, we want our graduate students to discover habits of mind and a disposition in the classroom that will help them connect with children and affect their learning," says Bowman.

Gordon's Teacher Residency Program is a natural extension of the school's mission, which seeks to inspire joyful learning, engage intellectual leadership, foster an empathic spirit and stimulate drive for a positive societal impact.

"Dr. Cooke was progressive, and we are progressive," said Wales. "We have stayed true to our course, even under persistent pressure to alter it. During times when our broader world was struggling, our numbers would drop. Yet, even as things became tight, the school persevered, communicating its message with purity and clarity."

Consider this letter from Board Chair Otto Hoffer in 1960 to Headmaster Larry Miller:

History

My feeling about our young people is that they should be capable of leading rich and rewarding lives, that their reservoir of emotional and intellectual wealth should enable them to contribute to their surroundings in a way which would create joy going out and coming back to them. The result would be, I should hope, the kind of inner contentment that resists compulsions and destructive illusions. The best kind of education is not forged by the hammer and anvil. It grows on the vine.

In partnership with students and their families, Gordon is that vine. It continues to grow and extend both its roots and its tendrils, reaching deeper and farther into an ever-widening community.

One hundred years after two children sat at small wooden desks in a Providence living room, Dr. Cooke's vision remains at the core of her school's philosophy. With more than four hundred students engaged in rigorous academic challenge, breathing the fresh air, and learning to see the humanity in all people, Gordon continues to "instill the spirit of joyous work," one child at a time.

The History chapter was written by Noah Davis '97.

The "all-school photo" taken in the fall of 2009.

Spaces

At Gordon's original home on Angell Street, the windows remained open year-round to promote physical health and keep young minds alert and ready to learn.

ntimate, cozy and inviting… these words were often used to describe Gordon's first home on the East Side of Providence. When the school outgrew its quarters and moved to an expansive site in East Providence, students quickly embraced the child-focused building designed by architect William Warner. Over the years, as the campus evolved, the focus on child-friendly architecture remained central to design decisions.

> A nice little building all along,
> Away from the noise and crowd,
> Where we will study the whole year through;
> That is what we have vowed.
>
> – By a sixth grade boy, from the January 1919 issue of *The Gordonian*

GORDON SCHOOL

The Gordon library in the Wallace House during the 1940s.

A Walking Tour of "Old Gordon"
This piece, written by a middle schooler, appeared in the March/April 1934 issue of *The Gordonian*.

Let me take you on a visit around Gordon. We will first visit a village that the kindergarten made. They have a church, a store, a library, a house and a barn. They made the grocery wagon and constructed the buildings. One-half of the first grade are studying the steps of transportation and the other half are studying about the Eskimos. They have made illustrated books about them.

Our next visit is to the second grade who takes us back to the cavemen and tree-dwellers. They have just finished Japan and there are some lovely pictures of Japanese life on the walls. The third grade is making a sugar grove. The fourth grade takes us on a Mediterranean cruise. They are also making May baskets to send to some old ladies.

Then we go to the Wallace House to the fifth grade who tell us the story of cotton. They are writing a play in connection with their project. The boys show us the cotton gin they made.

The sixth grade shows us the stained glass windows they made to use in the chapel in their room. A map of Asia is in progress in the seventh grade room. Others in that class are busy on friezes which represent the development of a modern industry. In the studio we see an Indian village being made by the eighth grade class.

One of the things we noticed especially about your school, perhaps because it is so different from ours, is the way you work and play in separate buildings and go from one to the other. It must be nice to get outdoors for a few minutes between classes.

– 1933, from a student visiting Gordon

The back porch and grape arbor on the pathway behind 405 Angell Street.

GORDON SCHOOL

Students at work in classrooms of the 1920s (above) and 1940s (below).

Do You Remember When?

When I place myself back at the old school campus between Waterman and Medway Streets in Providence, it is out-of-doors where I most often find myself… racing down the tricycle runway behind kindergarten's classroom, lining up along Medway's crowded sidewalk waiting to cross over to the graveled, hilly playground, practicing with my friends as one of the Friar Tucks (well stuffed with pillows) underneath Gordon's huge canopy of trees for an outdoor production of *Robin Hood*. I remember, too, the warmth of indoor classes and of teachers who knew and respected us. Trust is a hard-won commodity these days. At Gordon, it was the groundwork of everything we set out to do.

John Spicer '38, *Alumni Connection*, spring 1999

Spaces

Two friends enjoy outdoor play in the 1920s.

The Need for a New Gordon

From the 1960 Gordon publication, *Accent on the Child*

One morning, during Gordon's second decade, Dr. Cooke's husband opened the door to his dressing room, only to find a kindergarten class there. Marching downstairs in his dressing gown, the august gentleman confronted his wife and in tones of complete exasperation declared: "Helen, this has got to stop!"

Today, almost everyone would agree with him, for not only has Gordon School taken over the good gentleman's dressing room, but it has spilled over into every other available space as well. In the last three decades alone, the school has expanded from its first location at 405 Angell Street into an adjoining large frame house, a stable which is now used for a gymnasium and classrooms, a kindergarten and nursery building, and a converted shed.

Originally, every avenue was investigated and every effort made to keep Gordon at its present site. This, however, has proved impossible. After a thorough investigation of the available land in Greater Providence, the Board of Governors has selected a spacious seven-acre wooded site in East Providence as the new home for the Gordon School.

Here, on land ideally suited for its purposes, will be built an entirely new educational plant for Gordon, complete with a modern one-story integrated school structure and a more than ample variety of playing fields and other recreational facilities.

GORDON SCHOOL

Construction underway in 1962 at the new campus in East Providence.

We are at the crossroads of great events at our school. There are dazzling visions of a sturdy, modern, airy building surrounded by much green space with trees and playing fields and a brook to enjoy. This, we hope, is the future.

– Otto Hoffer, Board Chair, announcing the campaign for the East Providence campus, 1961

Spaces — Gordon School

A Child-Sized School Village For Children

The Providence Sunday Journal
January 13, 1963
By James K. Sunshine, former Board Chair and parent of Catherine '67 and Thomas '73

For one reason or another – usually lack of money – most new schools today come out looking like factories. One that didn't opened last week in the woods off South Broadway in East Providence. It is the new home for the Gordon School, a warm, wooden village of child-sized classrooms in which every effort was made to "make the children feel this was their school."

Architect William Warner, building his first school, knew little of the more customary flat-roofed modern variety except that he did not like their "glazed institutional corridors and electric devices" and did not think children really liked them either.

To get another effect, Mr. Warner used heavy wood beams and pine planking, thick concrete piers with the texture of the wood forms deliberately left imprinted ("something they could touch and feel"). The entire school is built to a child's scale, with small rooms and unusually low ceilings, but in the classrooms themselves the low walls give way to peaked roofs that soar up to 14 feet to give a feeling of space.

The main entrance bears the mark of the "owners," a 12-foot frieze of richly colored tiles made by the children last year and built into the wall by the delighted architect. Overhead, in defiance of electronics, there is an old school bell cast in Providence in 1814. A heavy white bell-rope dangles down from the wheel, and in the nearby office of Headmaster Laurance P. Miller, there is a hooked stick with which to catch it and pull it.

Inside, the school is splashed with color. On each classroom door the grade number is painted as high as a four-year-old is tall for easy reading. Outside, the nursery playground is guarded not by a fence but by a circular freeform embankment of earth that becomes on demand a fort, a parade ground, a slide or a spot for King-of-the-Mountain. High boulders have been left around the campus for climbing and hide-and-seek, and every classroom looks out upon the woods, the stream and the spring-fed pond.

A student rings the school bell, cast in Providence in 1814, at the East Providence campus.

The current campus at 45 Maxfield Avenue, now occupying twelve acres with 73 percent open space.

I had a favorite nook in the library where I used to curl up and read whenever I could. I discovered my love for history in that library.
– Ted Widmer, '76

Students from the 1970s and 1980s discover cozy reading spaces within the Arthur Livingston Kelley Library.

Spaces
Gordon School

The Joukowsky Family Library, which opened in 2002, houses more than 17,000 volumes including one of the most extensive collections of books for young adult readers in the area. Weekly classes, book clubs, reading games, competitions and the "Gordoncott Medal" instill a love of reading at an early age.

A Library in the Heart of the School

Architect Randall Imai reflects on his experience designing the Joukowsky Family Library.

When we first came to interview for the job, the interviews were in what used to be Mrs. Whinery's room, the highest room in the Middle School. It was dark and I looked out the window across the rooftops of the rest of the school and could see the little glow from the skylights of each room. We looked out to where the library would be and it was funny. This is a strange image, but the image I had of the future library was a merry-go-round. In other words, it was something that was turning, and it was a center of activity, because in my most romantic thinking, a library is something that should be the center of the school.

Two ideas that the librarians wanted to include had been features in the old library. One was the reading corner that was stepped down into the floor. The other thing they wanted – and I couldn't understand this – was a really small space. The space we decided on was underneath the stairs. When I came in the first day of school and saw the pillows tossed all around inside I could see it was a great idea.

Sunlight and a child-friendly design characterize the school's home in East Providence.

GORDON SCHOOL

When the Middle School building opened in 1970, the "well" became a popular feature, with stairs ascending toward a cathedral ceiling and a casual space for relaxing with friends.

Open classrooms in the late 1960s and early 1970s reflected a trend in progressive education toward a team-teaching plan organized by divisions rather than grades. The spaces occupied by the open classrooms pictured here now comprise several classrooms.

Gordon teachers don't impose learning — they enable it by making school a place where students explore their own interests. Students leave Gordon regarding study not as an obligation, but as a source of endless possibility.
— Diane Genereux '92

Spaces

Lynn Bowman teaches in a Middle School classroom in the 2000s.

Santana Sluss engages Kindergarteners during circle time.

Today's classrooms allow space for students to discover their distinct methods of organization.

GORDON SCHOOL

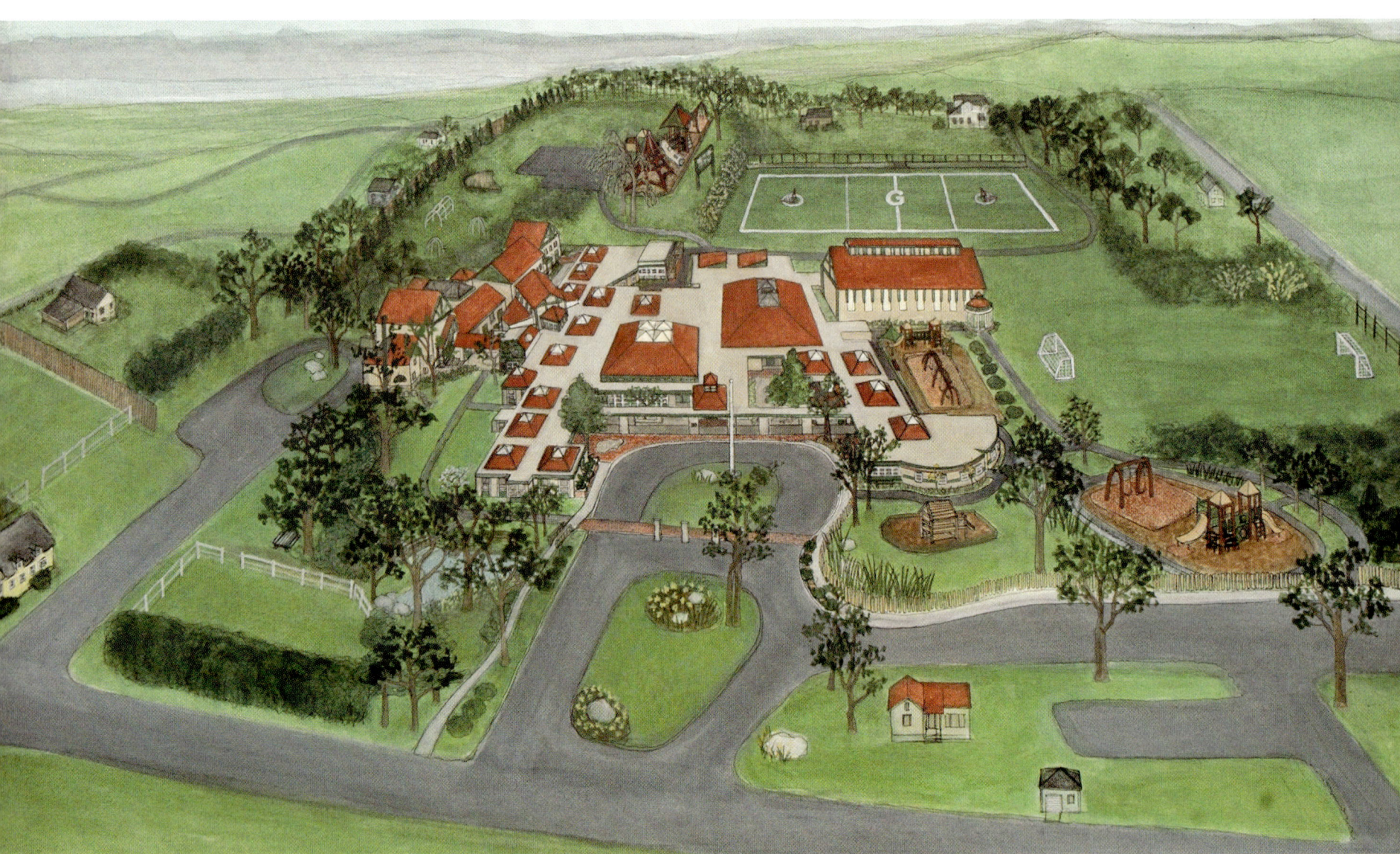

The East Providence campus, painted in 2008 by Noelle Walters, a teacher in the Lower School.

Spaces

Several years ago I came back to Gordon to pick up my niece, Samantha. As she showed me around the school, we came across the tiles in the first grade hallway. To my astonishment, we found the tile that I designed during my 1979-80 school year. I had not remembered doing it until that moment. As I stood there, all my memories of the arts program at Gordon came rushing back to me.
– Susanna Rhodes Beckwith '84, Trustee and parent of Isabelle '14, Lila '16 and Posey '20

GORDON SCHOOL

As part of their classroom studies, Middle School students calculate their ecological footprint. Their research includes experiments conducted at the pond and in natural environments throughout the twelve-acre campus.

Pond Project

This *Providence Journal* article from Nov. 18, 1977 describes one of many projects centered on the Gordon pond.

The man walked over and asked no one in particular what the kids were doing. "They're building a dam," he was told. The eleven youngsters at the Gordon School on Maxfield Avenue were taking their little project very seriously.

Some were busy mixing concrete that was being poured into the wooden forms spanning the south end of the tiny spring-fed pond in front of the school. Others were tamping the concrete in place, and occasionally, at the urging of David Wells, their instructor, a few would grab pails and begin bailing out water that was seeping under a temporary earth dam that held back the current from the forms.

Wells said the dam will have a moveable center portion that can be opened and closed so that the depth of the water can be regulated.

"This is going to be a big help in studying the ecology of the pond," he said.

(Left) The "mushrooms" on the East Providence campus double as an outdoor classroom space and recreation area. (Above) At Gordon's old home on Angell Street, students test their balance.

GORDON SCHOOL

Gordon now sports three distinct playgrounds for different ages and abilities.

Spaces

The athletic area near the Wallace House on Medway Street (right) demonstrated Dr. Cooke's commitment to physical health. Years later, Gordon's new facility would feature the Bradford Badger Munsill Gymnasium (bottom right), and more recently, the state-of-the-art Nelson Field House (below).

Learning

As Gordon enters its second century, the school remains true to its progressive roots. From preschool children learning to grow and cook their own food, to fourth graders reading immigrant stories, to eighth graders who test their knowledge in the real world through service learning, Gordon challenges students to reach for excellence. Gordon's multicultural curriculum fuels each child's innate curiosity and idealistic spirit, preparing them to enter a complex and diverse world.

In Gordon's early days, a station wagon driven by teachers served as the school bus. Now, hundreds of children travel from all over Rhode Island and nearby Massachusetts to attend Gordon every day.

ACADEMICS

EARLY CHILDHOOD

We loved the school and were happy there, and that was not mere chance, as I learned when I went later to other schools. From the beginning, Dr. Cooke felt that children should be happy and healthy in their work. She made our environment healthful and attractive and she gave us wonderful teachers, whom we loved devotedly and found interesting. That does not seem remarkable to us now, but it was then.

– Hope Cary Branch '17, *The Gordon School Story*

Students start by mastering basic skills, the building blocks of learning. (Below, center) Early Childhood Director Maureen Kelly welcomes a student.

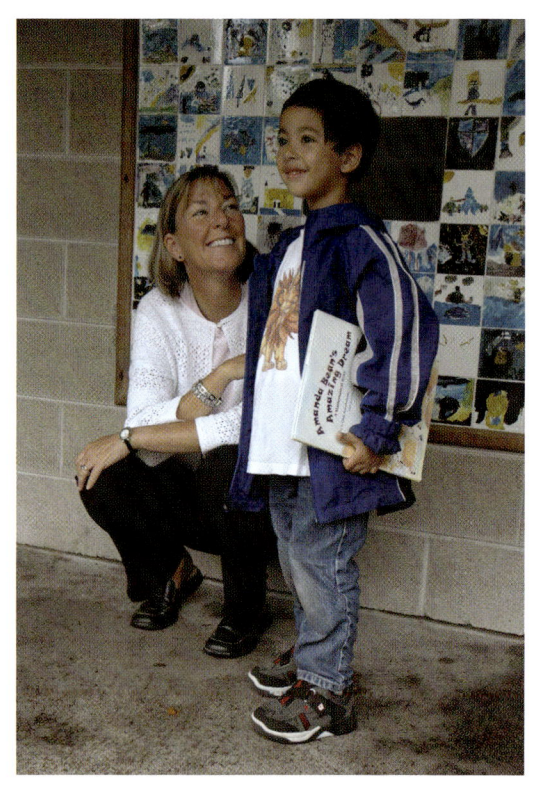

Learning

Our son, who had never attended school, now asks me to drive faster so he can get to Gordon. We know he is happy, secure and learning in an exciting environment, and that puts us at ease.

– Gordon parent

Building a sense of community begins on the first day of school and continues throughout a student's experience at Gordon.

Blossoms

By Beth Ruttenberg '76,
from the 1975 edition of *Myriad*

Blossoms are like people
opening up to a new year
to begin again
to say hello to the world.

The trees are whistling,
the flowers are swaying,
the birds are chirping.
all is quiet except
the natural sounds of nature.

Life is like the earth
rotating around in circles,
for new generations keep
appearing to take over
the old generation.

A group of Gordon's younger students, May 1938.

Gordon's campus includes two large gardens, maintained by students as part of the curriculum. These organic gardens, fueled by school compost and watered by a runoff rainwater barrel system, produce healthy snacks for students.

I remember feeling emotionally safe at Gordon. This was true for me and my classmates, and this comfort level improved our education. I learned better and gained self-confidence. At Gordon today, I see so many students developing into confident, independent young people.

—Jennifer Friedman Schnirman '81,
parent of Ruby '13 and Leah '17

Learning

Preschoolers at work in the 1980s (below) and in the 2000s (bottom). Shanon Connor (left) encourages her Preschool students.

Primary Happenings
From the March 1972 edition of *The Gordon Gazette*

Over the past several weeks, P1 [nursery] children have been learning about animals that hibernate, how magnets are used, who our presidents have been and are, names and appearances of shapes, and how sounds are made, both by humans and animals.

The P2 [kindergarten] children have been making their own books, dictating and illustrating stories, collecting cards of words as they master them, then making books of sentences using those words.

In sciences, the P2 children have finished a weather booklet – formulas, weather cycles, thermometers, weather words, poems, drawings – and they have painted a beautiful mural inspired by the Providence weather. Also, they are working on a transportation booklet including cut-out examples of transportation from the earliest times till the present. On Wednesdays, they have a free day when they can pursue their own interests. Among other things, they have baked jelly cakes, decorated bottles and created a fanciful marshmallow zoo.

GORDON SCHOOL

(Above) Teacher Victoria Tolbert with a Nursery student. (Below) Fran Bidwell reads to her Kindergarteners.

Early Childhood students develop skills that will open doors of discovery for them throughout their years at Gordon.

Learning

Katherine B. Kronquist and her Kindergarten students in the 1940s.

At the Gordon School we believe in youth, in the individual and in helping the child to build the right habits and attitudes, even an interest in disciplining himself so that the child takes the pioneer's joy in doing hard things well.

– 1935 edition of *The Gordonian*

Young Kindergarten students studying Alaska pose for this photo, to be carried by a musher during the Iditarod Great Sled Race.

GORDON SCHOOL

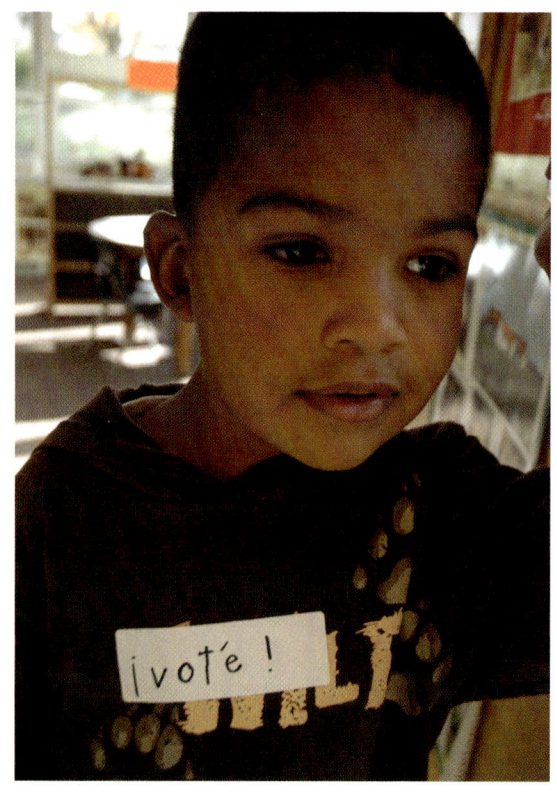

Citizenship begins in the early years, with opportunities to raise funds for important causes and the privilege of voting, even if the choice is simply between sprinkles and syrup on your ice cream.

Prior to winter break, Kindergarten students make popcorn, bag it, and sell it to members of the school community to raise money for mittens and hats for local children in need.

Learning

ACADEMICS

LOWER SCHOOL

Louise Burbank (upper left) assists a second grade student; Faythe Herdrich (above) reads to her first grade class.

Dinosaur Goes to School

From the November 13, 1972 edition of *The Providence Journal*

The dinosaur, that extinct beast that lived anywhere from "110 to 18 million years ago," has been enjoying a second childhood recently at the Gordon School in East Providence where first graders have been papering their way back into prehistoric times.

"I wasn't really expecting a dinosaur," Billy Markel, 6, of "Providence, RI, 02906" said of the approximately ten-foot long and six-foot-high Tyrannosaurus Rex that has been taking shape over the last week in the classroom.

Billy noted that the real thing was not made of paper strips, chicken wires and two Christmas bulbs for eyes.

"That isn't a real dinosaur because all that he has in himself is rock so he'll be balanced." Billy paused there and took stock. "I said a lot of things, didn't I?" he beamed.

A lot of first graders have been saying a lot of things lately, responding with delight to the project conceived by their science teacher, Mrs. Meredith Howe.

"It's kind of hard to imagine a prehistoric world for kids," said Mrs. Howe, who originally tried to get some dinosaur bones to illustrate the prehistoric studies.

When that failed she decided to turn to the papier-mâché that Gordon students use frequently. "We figure each year we do something bigger and better," Mrs. Howe said.

The dinosaur began taking shape in the living room of Mrs. Medro Marcal, whose son, Pedro, is a student in the class. Mrs. Howe and Mrs. Marcal did the preliminary shaping of the chicken wire before bringing Rex to the classroom where he is gathering layers of paper strips and dozens of fans.

"I like the dinosaur a lot," Pedro said. "He's the strongest meat-eating animal. Back in the old days it was hard to make them and now it's hard to study about them."

Pedro and his classmates have been learning to distinguish between meat-eating and plant-eating dinosaurs and have traced their reign in history from their beginnings to their unfortunate end.

"It rained and got cold," Michael Baum, 6, of Boylston Avenue, explained of the dinosaurs' demise. "Got real cold and stuff and they couldn't live. Some didn't catch cold. Some ate each other and stuff."

Learning

Carol Crout with her second grade students.

After Kindergarten, students encounter an increasingly rigorous curriculum.

47

Stretching the Limits

Written in 2009 by Peyton Gibson, Trustee, and Carol Gibson, parents of Rachel '05 and Caleb '14

Gordon is a special place that both nurtures and challenges children and their families. The challenge comes when Gordon stretches the limits of our understanding of the world we live in and asks us to question traditional norms of behavior, especially when it comes to issues concerning social justice and equity.

We tell each other quite frequently how fortunate we are to be part of the Gordon community—a community where we are asked to be a partner in our child's education and not just an observer. We hope that we express this by our involvement and our day-to-day interactions with others in the Gordon community.

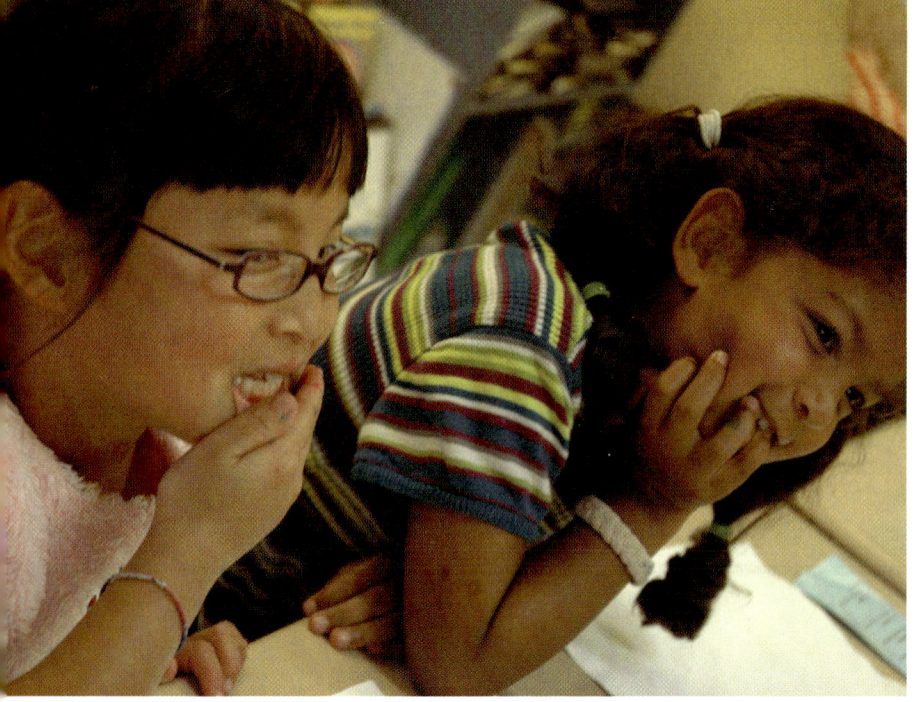

Learning

Third Grade Rights & Responsibilities

Using the "United Nations Declaration of the Rights of a Child" as a launching pad, third graders generate a list of rights and responsibilities as they widen their knowledge of what it means to expect and receive kindness from each other, while serving as role models to their Preschool and Nursery buddies. Here's what they came up with in 2009:

Every third grader has the right …
- to have a teacher from whom he or she can learn
- to be called by his or her name (or what he or she prefers to be called)
- to not be bullied
- to have a friend
- to feel part of a class
- to feel welcome
- to have a safe school
- to be treated equally
- to be different
- to be handicapped
- to be trusted
- to feel encouraged
- to play
- to have a goal

Every third grader has the responsibility …
- to be a good friend
- to include others
- to behave in a way that will prevent others from getting hurt
- to be encouraging to others

In a 1928 edition of *The Gordonian*, students (pictured right) share their thoughts about the care packages they have prepared for children in war-torn France: "This Christmas a good many of us will have to content ourselves with a few simple gifts, so that we shall be able to send clothes, money and food to the poor homeless children across the seas in France."

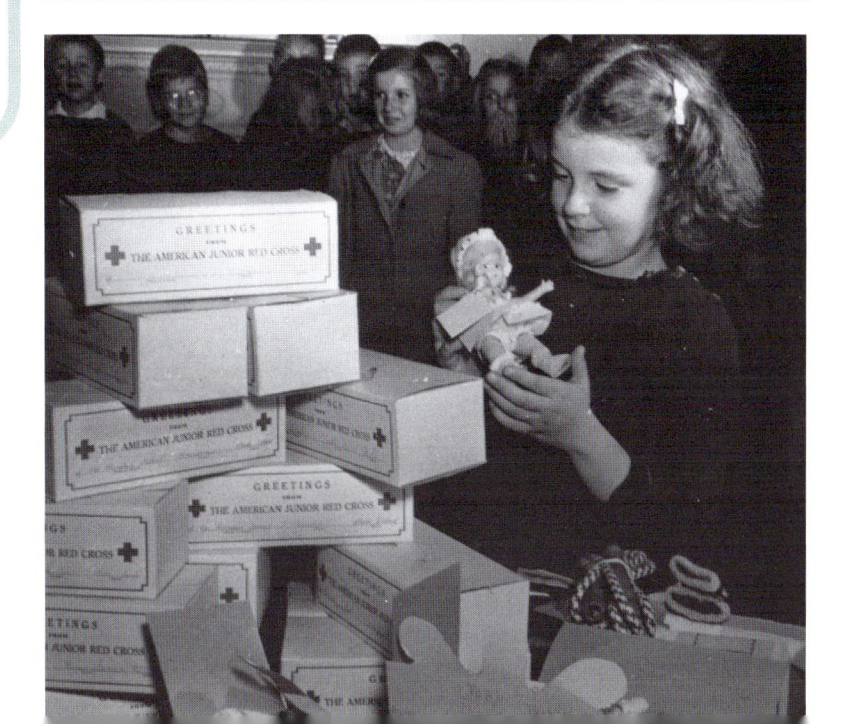

Miss Edith Childs with her final fourth grade group at Gordon, 1963.

Edith Childs ... An Appreciation
From the Gordon newsletter, July 1964, by Mary B. Trask, Director of the Elementary Division,
on Edith Childs' retirement after forty years of teaching

One of the third graders finally caught up with the news: Miss Childs wasn't going to teach fourth grade next year. Miss Childs wasn't going to be at Gordon.

"What will they do?" he asked. Then, answering himself, "I s'pose, just not have fourth grade. Just skip it."

To most of us, as to that third grader, it seems impossible that there can be fourth grade at Gordon School without Edith Childs.

Perhaps we had better, as that third grader proposed, just skip the fourth grade if Miss Childs isn't going to be here to teach it. But perhaps, since the terms "Edith Childs" and "Gordon School" seem to be synonyms, we would do better to hope – no, to believe and make sure – that, even with Edith not in one of the classrooms, Gordon School will still be the place where success is recognized and applauded, where finding one's place in the world, happily, is still considered more important than any other easily measurable success.

Learning

I've learned that when it's more fun for the kids, it's more fun for me, too. Over the years, the best part of teaching has remained the same: the kids. They're just as curious, just as eager to learn. Second grade is a year of learning the basics – reading, writing, math. The biggest change may be the materials we use to teach the basics. They're much richer and more interesting now.
– Dotty Thornley, Lower School teacher, 1979-2007

(Below left) Minna Ham with her first grade class; (below right) Librarian Frances Martindale (left) and Dotty Thornley share the excitement of reading with students.

GORDON SCHOOL

The personal connection between student and teacher can take you anywhere.
– Barbara Hendrie, Trustee and parent of
Will '94, John '97 and David '02

(Above) Pat Jennings with a fourth grade student.

Learning

Cendhi Arias with a second grade student (top left).

It is a courageous kind of learning that is fostered at Gordon. Each child feels the adult expectation of engagement. The children soon realize that at Gordon, the ability to step into the most confounding questions is honored and valued.

-- Ralph Wales, Head of School,
1994 - present

GORDON SCHOOL

Gordon students encounter nature directly through the school's hands-on curriculum.

Earth Week

From the May 1972 edition of *The Gordon Gazette*

Having read an article on Earth Week in our weekly newspaper and what was being done around the country, Mrs. Rice's class held an extensive discussion on their views and ideas. Then each child wrote a letter to a government official expressing his ideas.

Dear Governor Licht,

Earth is our only home. We must care for it. I am working on a perpetual motion machine to go into the motor of my hovercraft. I am going to try to harness up a radiometer to force pressure through turbines on the other side of it. If it works, it could change the world. I am going to try to patent it. Please try to help me get a patent. I am only ten and they might discriminate against me, but I know you are very fair and that's why I wrote you. As you go through my letter you might wonder about mass production but I say Ford can do it, we can do it. You might think I'm a little weird and so do I but personally I think it's a good idea.

Sincerely yours,
Erik Urdang, Age 10
(Class of 1976)

Learning

Janet Burnham (left) and Diana Reeves explore the wonders of language and literature with their third grade classes.

Peace

By Sam Yelnosky, 3rd grade, 2009

Peace tastes like matzah ball soup
   or potato latkes.
Peace smells like my dad's garden
   and grandma's rhubarb pie.
Peace feels like happiness
   and a warm bed.
Peace sounds like laughter
   and water crashing on a beach.
Peace looks like the Mad River Valley
   or a sunset after a long day.

GORDON SCHOOL

I still miss the intimate nature of Gordon. I miss knowing everyone's name, having class with my entire grade and feeling at home in the hallways walking to Lower School gym class with Mr. Cruise. The fact that every teacher cares about the learning process of every student is something that Gordon does exceptionally well.
   – Ben Freedman '01, in the Winter 2006 *Alumni Connection*

Learning

ACADEMICS

MIDDLE SCHOOL

Entering Middle School is a major milestone for a Gordon student. For years, younger students look up, physically and intellectually, to these leaders of the community. Middle School students serve as mentors, role models and inspiration for their counterparts in Lower School and Early Childhood. As students pass this final threshold, they know it is their turn to accept the responsibilities and privileges that come with being the senior members of their school.

GORDON SCHOOL

Arnold Look conducts class (upper left) in the cramped fifth grade classroom at Wallace House during the early 1960s. Mercedes Quevedo (upper right) teaches Middle School in the late 1970s; Carlos Isidoro (lower left) teaches foreign language, and Samantha Kravitz (lower right) works with her fifth grade students in the 2000s.

Learning

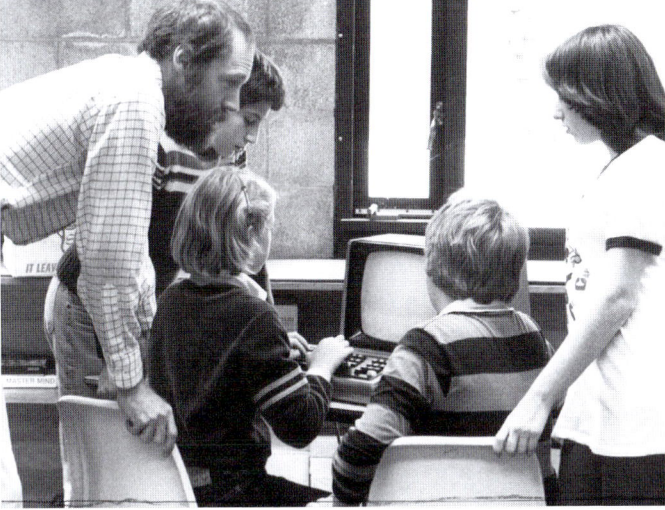

Computers became a familiar sight on the Gordon campus during the 1980s. Students work with William Fritzmeier (upper right) in 1983; Shai Pina (upper left) conducts class in the computer lab in 2009.

Gordon is a place where you learn how to learn. If you've learned well, you can go anywhere and do anything.

– George Greenhalgh '39,
parent of Nancy Greenhalgh Larkin '65
and David Greenhalgh '68

GORDON SCHOOL

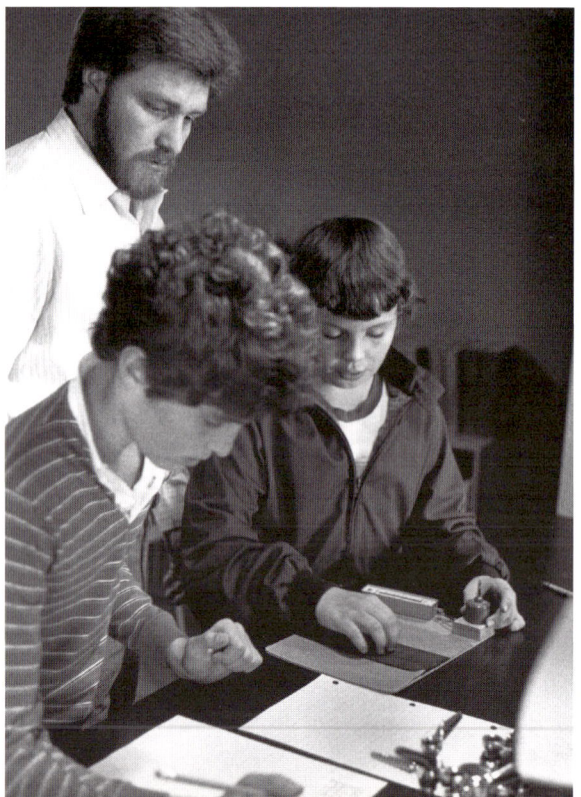

Sean Hamer with his seventh grade math and science class.

Carl Bishop with Middle School students in the 1980s.

Learning

Cynthia Spence helps sixth grade students discover their distinct voices as writers and thinkers.

Learning to Love My Driveway

Because it is so simple, yet useful
Because it takes me into different worlds
Because I don't need a passport to enter
Because it is my own
Because it is full of memories
Because I tripped on the crack on the edge
Because I fell off my bike, riding for the first time on my own
Because I ran into the bush numerous times
Because I have put time and effort fixing it
Because I stayed out in the night to shovel snow, so my dad could get to work the next morning
Because my neighbor is too old to do it on her own
Because I could not feel my hands for the following hours
Because I beat my personal best
Because I stayed out in the rain to shoot hoops for the game tomorrow
Because I pitched a tennis ball against my garage until I made all-stars
Because I landed my first alley over the pile of bricks
Because it will always be there
Because I helped fill in gaps with cement
Because I cut the grass around it, and trim the hedges
Because I know that it is not only for me
Because we have problems with the car again
Because we need to fix the gutters on it
Because we had to take apart the snow blower
Because we wanted to put new roofing
Because there will always be needs and uses
Because our life constantly changes
Because time passes
While it is still my driveway
My driveway of dreams
My driveway of progression

By Randy Alsabe '10, age 13, 2009
Modeled off *Learning to Love America* by Shirley Geok-Lin Lim

GORDON SCHOOL

From Gordon's earliest days, teachers approached the study of ancient cultures through an immersion process. Decades past, students transformed their classroom into a Viking hall. Today, fifth graders spend a week transforming their classroom into a lifelike scene from ancient China, Egypt and India.

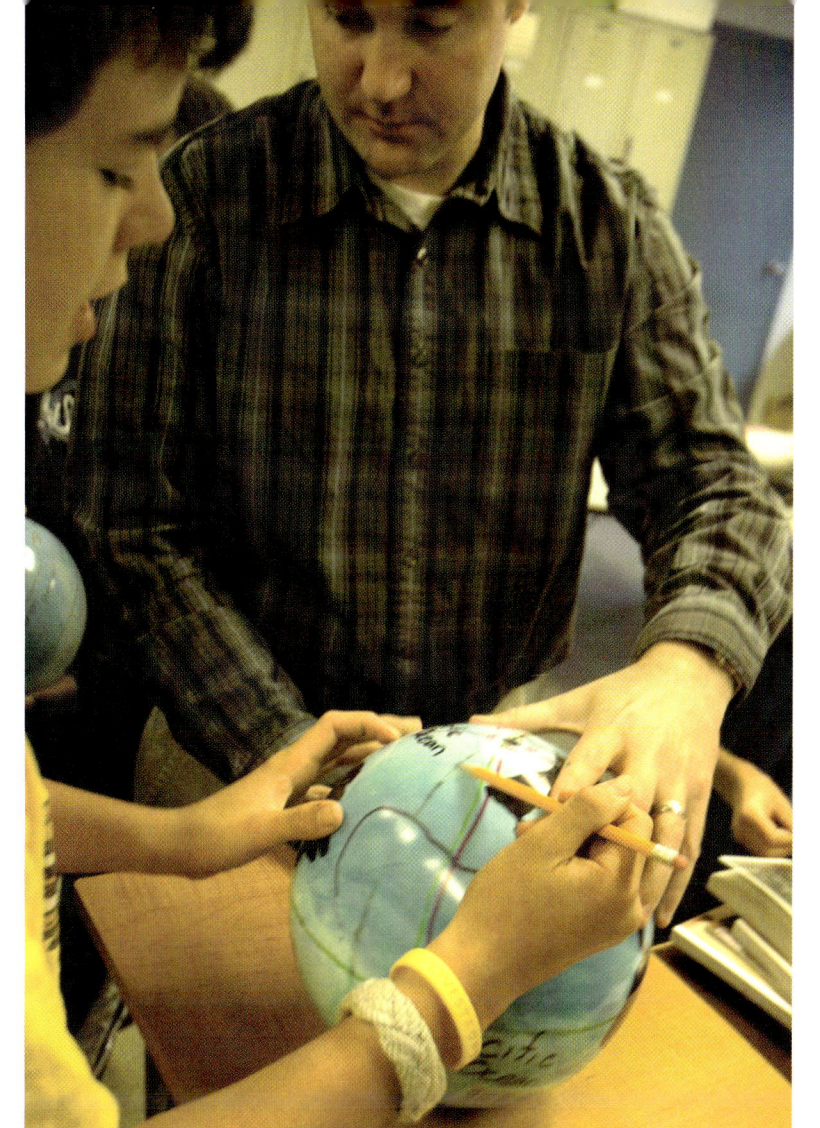

Learning

Greg Carson guides sixth grade students in preparing to create their memory maps.

Karan Takhar '05 took first place in the National Geographic Society's International Geography Bee in 2005.

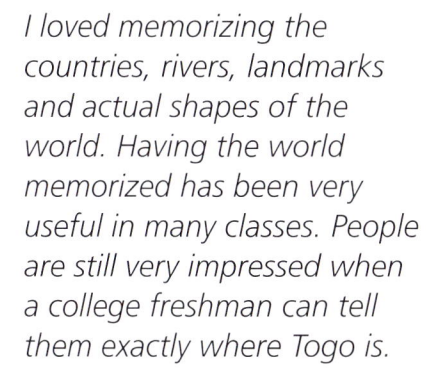

I loved memorizing the countries, rivers, landmarks and actual shapes of the world. Having the world memorized has been very useful in many classes. People are still very impressed when a college freshman can tell them exactly where Togo is.

– Sarah Reeves '96, from her 2006 Commencement address

Every Middle School student learns to draw a map of the world from memory, including every country and all major rivers, bodies of water, mountain ranges and many cities.

GORDON SCHOOL

Hands-on science at the East Providence campus.

Nature Study

From the January/February 1929 edition of *The Gordonian*

The fall nature work centered about specimens brought, for the most part, into class by the children.

In the fifth and sixth grades, leaves were examined, pasted into notebooks, labeled, and such interesting facts as could be gathered were written into the notebooks with the specimens. Later the corresponding twigs and bugs will be added to each page to complete the collection.

The seventh grade girls have been studying astronomy. To supplement the material in their texts, they have made notebooks containing pictures of the stars.

The lower grades learned about the various ways seeds have of distributing themselves, studied the main star-pictures of the heavens and found out something about the smaller fur-bearing animals. This last study included a lantern slide lecture.

The work will continue with further study of birds, animals, trees, etc. and in the spring it will be given especial point by expeditions to the park and elsewhere to observe the birds and to study the trees.

Learning

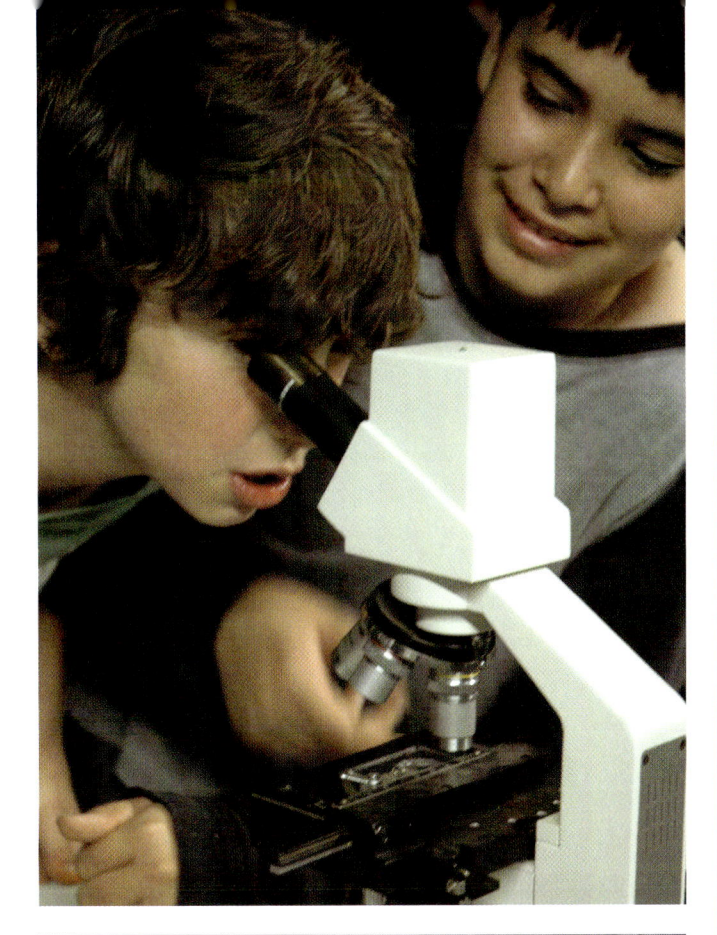

Librarian Karla Harry (right) conducts outdoor research with her students.

GORDON SCHOOL

Days in New Hampshire
By Adele Parker '79, reflecting on a field trip in the
1977 edition of *Myriad*

Red, yellow, orange, and brown
The colors of a tree from roots to crown.
The wind in the trees, the birds in the sky,
The insects that crawl, the insects that fly.
The pure clear spring water on the mountain,
As compared to the New Hampshire water from a fountain.
The Glen Course, the Southern Ropes,
The cider press and the bioscope.
Watching a beaver swim across the water,
And watching chipmunks, with no thought of slaughter.
Red, yellow, orange, and brown,
The colors of a tree from roots to crown.

Field trips have long been a part of the Gordon experience – a time for team building, nature appreciation and fun. From mountain hikes in New Hampshire to Cape Cod beaches, students establish a special bond with each other on these excursions.

Learning

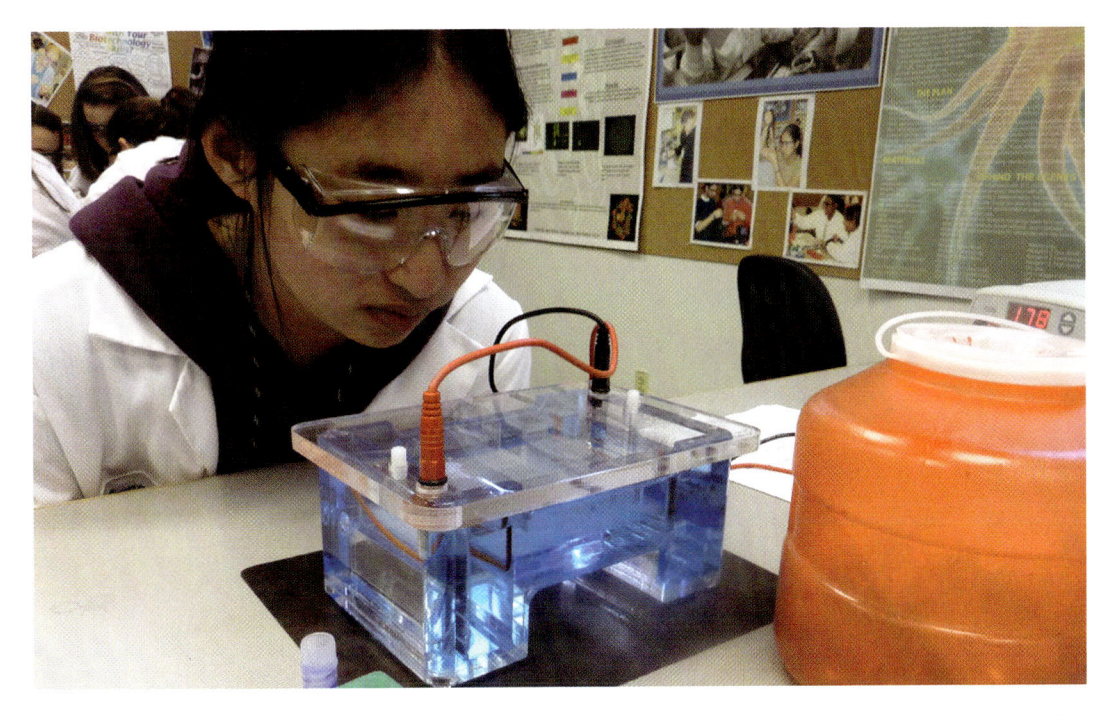

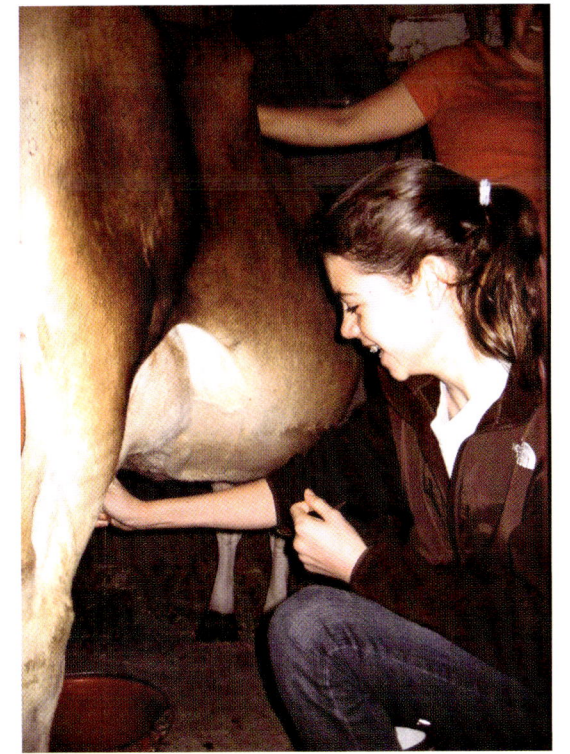

Recent day trips include visits to the Biogen/MIT Museum, Plimoth Plantation, New Bedford Whaling Museum, Caratunk Wildlife Refuge, Ellis Island, Apeiron Institute for Sustainable Living, Fogland Beach, McCoy Stadium, Mystic Aquarium & Institute for Exploration, Save the Bay Center, Old Sturbridge Village and the RISD Museum of Art.

67

GORDON SCHOOL

CIVIL RIGHTS STUDIES

The eighth grade's annual trip to Alabama and Georgia brings to life the students' classroom work. An endowed fund established in 2003 by Rick Bready (parent of Arika '02 and Max '03) and Sally Lapides (former Trustee and parent of Ian '99 and Emmett Barnacle '03) provides this life-changing experience.

It's amazing to think that only 45 years ago, Bloody Sunday happened right where we were. It took those marchers three tries to get over that bridge, and we got across with no trouble. We walked as free people. I think that is just incredible.
— Sylvia Skerry '10 from her Civil Rights Trip memory book

Students at Centennial Park in Atlanta, Georgia.

Learning

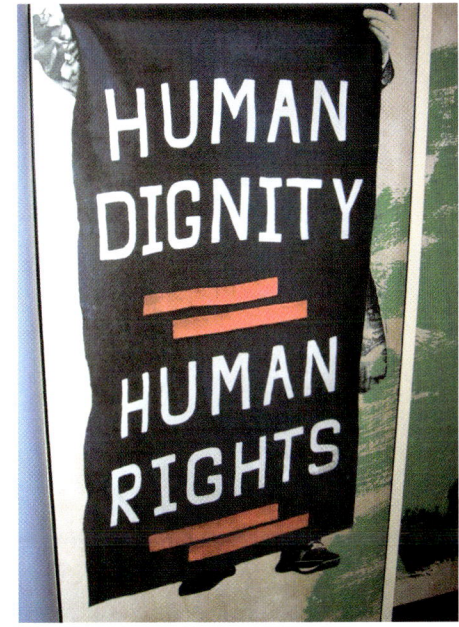

I will be a responsible leader in my everyday life, and especially at school. I will try to teach other people to fight for the things they believe in. I will help people when they are in need. Now that I know that all the small things can lead up to something big, I will try to keep doing those small things that nobody thinks to do.

– Michael Janigian '10 from his Civil Rights Trip memory book

GORDON SCHOOL

EXPERIENTIAL LEARNING

Carter Joseph ("C.J.") Buckley, a member of the class of 2000, inspired others with his empathy and desire to help others. To honor C.J.'s memory, his family (Lucy, Carter '52, and their daughter Helen Buckley Cappetta '94) and friends established the C.J. Buckley Fund for Experiential Learning, which provides children with opportunities to experience success as thinkers, learners and contributors, and thus to develop an awareness of their academic potential and personal abilities.

C.J. Buckley '00

Eric Polite, former Director of Diversity, and Martha Dineen Wales help fourth grade students raise the flag.

As Jim and I watch our children grow and mature into informed and active citizens we credit the outstanding foundation they have received as students of the Gordon School.

– Jim Watkins and Liz Pannell,
parents of Miles '04 and Graham '08

Learning

Eighth grader Jonathan Pabis '07 with his students at the Paul Cuffee School, during his service learning experience in 2007.

SERVICE LEARNING

Service learning begins at an early age at Gordon as fourth graders take responsibility for raising and lowering the flag with care and respect. Sixth graders manage the school's recycling efforts, visiting every classroom and office in the building twice a week to collect and sort recyclables. Eighth grade students step outside the classroom walls and experience first-hand the agencies, schools and individuals that help others in Rhode Island communities. Genesis Center, Amos House, Highlander School, Trailside Daycare and the Paul Cuffee School are among the organizations where students spend every morning for a month working and learning.

A Personal Awakening

Maura Davis McAuliffe '88, reflecting on her experience at the Genesis Center.

The children were resting for naptime as Marilyn walked around the room checking on the kids. She told me something that really made me think. The family of a little girl that I adored was having many problems.

The family came from Southeast Asia a few years ago, with ten children ranging from age one to nineteen. The mother speaks very little English but is very intelligent. The father speaks hardly any English and has just been laid off from his job. There is absolutely no money coming in for the family. The family has to depend on others for clothing and food.

Marilyn said the family had been through much tougher problems before they came to the United States. The mother pulls the family through all the difficulties. I don't know how she does it, but I really look up to a person like her.

It really made me think about how lucky I am. I think about how I get upset because I can't get things I want, and how these little children are so grateful for a pair of torn shoes or a flower. This whole experience has really changed me.

GORDON SCHOOL

VISUAL ARTS

Each year, opportunities for creative expression blossom in new ways at Gordon. The joyful scribbles of a young mind become refined and thoughtful pieces of art crafted with care.

72

Learning

Visual art teachers Dorothy Greenough (center) and Antoinette Downing (right) pictured in the art studio in the Wallace House.

(Above) Visual art teacher Gino Conti created an inspiring space in the old Wallace House building during the 1950s. Today's art studios encourage children to explore many forms of creative expression.

Visual art teachers Amy Cohen (left) and Toni Dumville (above) in the fine arts wing at the East Providence campus.

GORDON SCHOOL

2003 Visiting Artist Allison Newsome

Visiting Artists

Over the years, many families have chosen to support the arts at Gordon by establishing endowed funds. The Britt Nelson Fund brings students in direct contact with practicing visual artists through an annual artist-in-residence program.

Since its founding, the Britt Nelson Fund has brought the following artists to Gordon's classrooms:

1998 Painter Melissa Miller
1999 Glass artist Ursula Huth
2000 Storyteller and illustrator Baba Wagué Diakité
2001 Architect Roddy Langmuir
2002 Textile artist Jeung Hwa Park
2003 Sculptor Allison Newsome
2004 Sculptor Kitty Wales
2005 Photographer Marian Roth
2006 Puppeteers Dusan Petran and Aniece Novak
2007 Designer Gunnel Sahlin
2008 Painter and printmaker Joseph Norman
2009 Sculptor Ben Anderson, illustrator Amy Bartlett Wright and illustrator Julie Ann Collier
2010 Illustrator Bert Kitchen

2009 Visiting Artist Ben Anderson

An early art show at Wallace House.

Learning

Student artwork takes center stage at annual art shows, just as it did in years past at Gordon.

I like painting because I have an amazing teacher who inspires me to try new things. Right now I am working with watercolors, and I have improved my technique tremendously.

– Middle School student

She *may* be right. . . .

This fictitious letter from a concerned parent appeared as a spoof in the March/April 1931 Gordonian *from "Mrs. May B. Wright."*

Dear Mrs. Cooke:

My daughter, Eliza Jane, has been telling me some things about school which I do not approve of. To think that you teach painting to all your pupils! It is alright for the boys to take it, because that's a job for a man, not a lady. Aside from that, I want Eliza to be a "cook." That is why I send her to the "Cooke" School. Another thing which bothers me is that this past winter my daughter took "tapping." Goodness only knows she is nervous enough without having her learn how to "tap" her feet in society.

One other matter, when my child is going to have her pictures taken, I will take them. I do not approve of that "Studio" which she visits so often.

Furthermore, it is perfectly alright for the boys to learn how to be firemen, but I do not wish Eliza Jane to learn that occupation as she never could run a fire engine. So in the future, please excuse my precious from taking the fire drills.

But there, I mustn't run on any longer. It is so easy to write to you, Mrs. Cooke, and I know you will understand that I do not mean to hurt your feelings.

Yours sincerely,
Mrs. May B. Wright

Learning

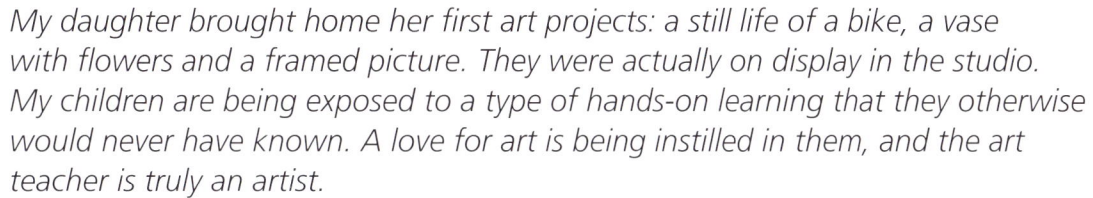

My daughter brought home her first art projects: a still life of a bike, a vase with flowers and a framed picture. They were actually on display in the studio. My children are being exposed to a type of hands-on learning that they otherwise would never have known. A love for art is being instilled in them, and the art teacher is truly an artist.

– Lower School parent

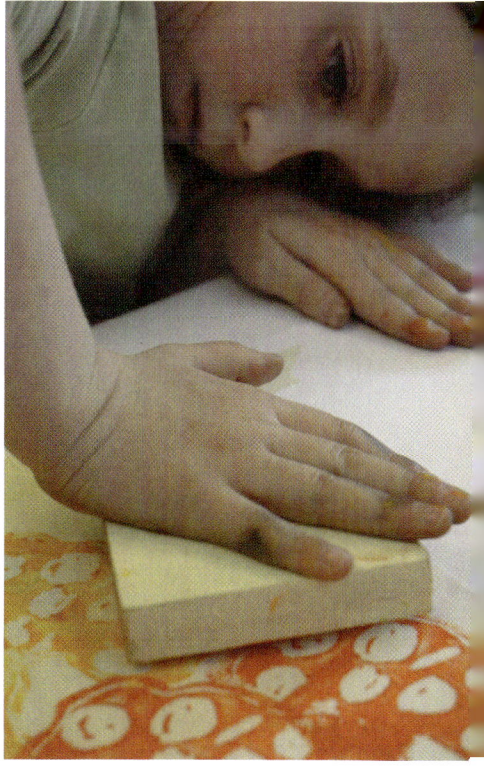

GORDON SCHOOL

PERFORMING ARTS

From a grassy lawn in the 1920s to the stage of the Activity Room in later decades, students learn to perform at an early age and develop confidence as the years progress.

I have been acting in plays since first grade when I was in Annie Jr. here at Gordon. From the moment I read my first two lines in a script, I was hooked. To this day, I still remember those lines and the fear and excitement of acting. Without those two lines, where would I be?
— Meghan Wales '10

Learning

Gordon School remains very special to me. It always felt as if I was traveling to a magical place with wonderful teachers and experiences that inspired my creativity and imagination.
— Rachel Thorne Germond '77

80

Learning

Every year, Lower and Middle School students present elaborate musicals and plays.

The Gordon School has long valued artistic self-expression in all its forms. Dramatic performance is particularly powerful because of the public nature of the experience. There is an open vulnerability that can be felt by those of us who watch. Young actors and actresses can be lifted to a new place of confidence and self-awareness as they experience success on the stage.

— Ralph Wales, Head of School, 1994 - present

GORDON SCHOOL

The performing arts are used throughout the Gordon curriculum to help realize the goal of producing students who are comfortable expressing themselves, verbalizing their thoughts in front of a group, and learning to view the world from perspectives other than their own.

Learning

A Monologue to Remember
By Jonah Parker '10 for the eighth grade's Centennial Time Capsule in 2010

I have decided that the object I will put into this time capsule will be the funny little prosthetic nose that I wore for my monologue from "Cyrano de Bergerac" this past fall. First of all, I love to act. I think that it is one of my greatest strengths, and I am very proud of what I have been able to achieve while doing it. It is something I want to continue with the rest of my life.

I don't think that I will ever forget what an amazing experience it was for me to do that monologue. I loved every second I was on stage. Even just wearing the costume was a blast. But I will never, ever forget the nose. When we open the time capsule in a few decades and I see it again, it will bring me back to some of the happiest moments in my childhood.

Jonah Parker '10

GORDON SCHOOL

MUSIC

It was my first grade music class here at Gordon which really sparked my desire to want to make music.

– Toria Rainey '10

Music is part of daily life at Gordon, as captured in a music class of the 1920s (lower left) and with music teacher Nancy Moore (lower right) in the 2000s.

Learning

(Above) Kindergarteners enjoy music class in the 1980s with Maggie Holmes (on guitar) and Ruth Winn (center, seated).

Music teacher Chrys Alam leading a choral group on guitar.

The last two years of my life have been some of the best for me. I have developed great friendships, confidence and a passion for music. I owe all of these to the decision to go to the Gordon School.

— Nick Mirza '07

GORDON SCHOOL

Young people are often told to follow their passion. That's important, but not as simple as it sounds. You may not know you're going to like something, or that it even exists, until you've been exposed to it. One's path is often guided by mentors, who can open doors by their own example.

— John Ravenal '73, in the Winter 2009 *Alumni Connection*

Learning

Music class in "the studio" at Wallace House (above, left and right) and a holiday concert at the East Providence campus in the 1960s.

What resonates with me now, as the mother of a young child, is the value that Gordon places on all the arts. The arts are an integral part of the curriculum at Gordon – as important as English and math – not lesser than, not more than, but equal to the rest of the Gordon experience.
— Susanna Rhodes Beckwith '84

GORDON SCHOOL

Music and drama students at Gordon benefit from the Ellen D. Grober Memorial Fund, the Peter Kaplan Memorial Fund and the Jonathan D. Arms Fund.

Learning

Band director Bill Beaudoin

Music teacher Lisa Stanziani Griffith

GORDON SCHOOL

HEALTH, WELLNESS & ATHLETICS

Children grow in their appreciation of team play, physical exercise and healthy life habits as they progress through Gordon's curriculum.

Learning

Bob McAdam (upper right) teaches students to dance; Jerry Cruise (lower right) teaches gymnastics.

Gordon taught me that learning is about team collaboration. I remember Gordon promoting this from early on in my education, and community learning is something that I still believe strongly in and promote in my daily life.

– Marjorie Markoff Warmkessel '68

GORDON SCHOOL

Head of School Frederick W. Locke gets into the action on Field Day at the East Side campus in the late 1950s.

Gordon provided a supportive environment for me to develop as a person and realize my own strengths. I was surrounded by classmates and teachers who believed in everything I did. In sailing, I concentrate on creating a supportive dynamic with my teammates by drawing upon what Gordon taught me – confidence, trust and a sense of self.

– Charlie Enright '98,
in the Fall 2006 *Alumni Connection*

Learning

Gordon coaches come from many corners of the Gordon community: (left to right, front row) Belle Sangalang, Kristen Fraza, Melissa Carman, Sean Hamer; (back row) Kevin Vartian, Becky Aitchison, Charlene Snyder, Caroline Thomas '01, Ryan McCoy.

On That Field
By Jillian DeStefano '10

On that field
looking straight ahead
seeing the girl sprinting
toward you.
Then she stops dead.
She looks up and glares,
two seconds pass,
she's still standing there.
But now,
you can see
my team and me
heading up the field
with the ball,
we shoot,
we score,
we win it all.

GORDON SCHOOL

Learning

The Greatest School in Town

This cheer, composed by the eighth grade class of 1932, is sung to the tune of "Freddy the Freshman."

Who has all the pupils,
The brightest bunch around?
Rah! Rah! It's Gordon!
The greatest school in town.
In acting, art and music,
Who has won renown?
Rah! Rah! It's Gordon!
The greatest school in town.
We came to get some knowledge
In Latin, French and math;
To read, to write, to draw,
And follow the straight path.
Who has all the pupils,
The brightest bunch around?
Rah! Rah! It's Gordon!
The greatest school in town.

GORDON SCHOOL

Learning

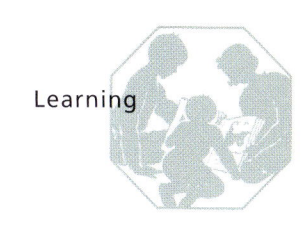

Charles Harrington teaches baseball in 1947.

Gordon's Engle Family Athletic Field raised Gordon's playing fields to the highest standards in 2006.

The most important thing about sports at Gordon is having fun, learning and being part of a team. These things are the core of the Gordon athletics sports program.

– Middle School student

Community

The word "community" characterizes Gordon more than almost any other. Over the years, Gordon has been nurtured by parents, students, alumni, teachers, staff, trustees and community leaders who believed in the work of the school. The "true spirit of joyous work" called for by founder Dr. Helen West Cooke does not begin or end at the classroom door; it is woven into the fabric of Gordon's ever-expanding community.

The tapestry that is Gordon will transcend any individual or moment in time.
– Darcey Hall, Head of School from 1985-1994

GORDON SCHOOL

FACULTY & STAFF
ARCHITECTS OF EDUCATION

Jane Anthony (right), who taught from 1941 to 1972, and her assistant, Louise Boyd, celebrate a birthday with their four-year-old students at the Angell Street campus.

Gordon teachers gather at an outing in 1939: (Standing left to right) Myra Manchester, Edith Childs, Winifred Rice, Elizabeth Fuller, Olga Hassell, Leonora Bennett; (kneeling) Evangeline Fachon; (seated) Celia Goodman, Gail Hodgman, Elizabeth Cooke and Erma Tulip.

Teachers from 1982, several of whom remain on the faculty in 2010: (front row, left to right) [not identified], Barbara Rehm, Dotty Thornley, Maggie Holmes, Linda Mullin; (second row) Mary Casale, Livia St. Florian, Tovia Siegel, Sue Smith, Maureen Kelly, Carroll Garland, Fran Bidwell; (back row) Denice Cardin, Jerry Cruise, Ruth Winn, Jean Comery-Hill, Linda Whitney, Mary Lou Cubbage, Harriet Wrenn.

Community

Norma Barsom-Morcos with a Nursery student in 2009.

(Right) Elizabeth Bakst watches the Founder's Day Assembly in 2010 with a preschool student.

Conversation with a Preschooler

This exchange took place between Owen Matheson, a preschooler in 2010, and his mother, Mandy Syers, and was included in a scrapbook for Owen's Preschool teacher Elizabeth Bakst on her retirement in 2010 after 25 years of teaching at Gordon.

Owen: Mrs. Bakst will never go to jail because she's so nice. She never steps on people in her class on purpose, anywhere on their body. I really do like her. She does like me a lot too. I like to talk with her a lot.

Mom: When you're a really old man, with gray hair and a long gray beard, what do you think you'll remember about Mrs. Bakst?

Owen: I don't know if I'll even have gray hair.

Mom: Well, what's something you'll remember about Mrs. Bakst your whole life, all the way 'til you're an old man?

Owen: Two things: That she likes to put the hot water and the cold water all the way on when she's washing her hands, same as me. Me and Mrs. Bakst agree that we like to do that when we're washing our hands. And we both love that little cute car. We imagine it looks like a Busytown car. We like to watch that car.

Mom: Let's pretend we're writing a letter to Mrs. Bakst. How would it go?

Owen: Dear Mrs. Bakst. I love you, Mrs. Bakst. We'll miss you, Mrs. Bakst. Love, Owen.

GORDON SCHOOL

Receptionist Kim O'Donnell

Assistant to Head of School Clare Blackmer

Lower School teachers from 2009: left to right, bottom row) Minna Ham, Sandy Goldberg, Diana Reeves, Janet Burnham, Toni Dumville, Chrys Alam, Pat Jennings; (second row) Kate Mercurio, Linda Mullin, Mimi Roterman, Jacqui Ketner, Noelle Walters, Afiya Samuel; (on pyramid, left to right) Frances Martindale, Melissa Carmen, Maryanne Pieri, Rosemary Colt, Cendhi Arias, Louise Burbank.

Martha Baker directs kitchen activities.

Community

Building and grounds staff Joe Machado (left) and Rob Howard install the Centennial banners.

Veodis Walker, maintenance staff and bus driver, joined Gordon in 1968.

Isabel and Dan Costa, maintenance staff, cook up hot dogs at Carnival in 1961.

Former Admission Co-Director Julie Cucchi bakes cookies with children.

103

GORDON SCHOOL

PARENTS ... THE STRENGTH BEHIND THE INSTITUTION

A History of Involvement

The first official parent organization at Gordon was founded in 1932, but parent involvement has been a constant from the school's earliest days. Over the last century, the Gordon Parent Association, which became the Gordon Community Association (GCA) in 1991, has supported the school in every conceivable manner.

From organizing lectures, activities and field trips to electing the school's first governing board in 1944, parents have taken an active interest in the life of Gordon. When the early building needed repairs or furniture needed to be painted, mothers and fathers rolled up their sleeves and got the job done. They hosted midways, markets, country fairs, hobby shows and more.

Through the years, parents developed creative ideas for fundraising to fuel the school's growth and mission. The first Carnival in 1957 went on to become one of the year's biggest fundraisers and most anticipated events. In the 1990s, parents conceived "Cooks & Books," later renamed "Hands Around the Table," which brought in celebrated chefs and authors for a festive evening while raising money for local organizations.

For many years, lunchtime has been a family affair at Gordon, with parents lending a hand in the kitchen, the serving table and behind the scenes. From bake sales and gift wrap fundraisers to major events, Gordon parents have contributed their skills and time willingly.

Parent volunteers have shelved countless books, organized impressive book fairs, and assisted in major community-building events, like 2004's "Communitas," a celebration of many cultural heritages. They have served on and chaired the Board of Trustees and have been strong advocates for a Gordon education. Recognizing the need to make a Gordon education available to a wider population, the GCA created the school's first financial aid endowment in 1992. In every corner of the Gordon community, parents have been the enduring strength behind the institution.

Robert Schacht, first president of the Gordon Parent Association, with Mrs. Gordon MacPherson in 1944.

Community

Gordon parents set excellent examples of community service for their children by lending a helping hand in many areas of the school.

Gordon parents helping out in the kitchen.

Gordon parents (l to r) Jane Joukowsky, Maraya Goff and Cheryl Nathanson at a Board of Trustees event in 2009.

GORDON SCHOOL

FIELD DAY

A year's worth of friend-making culminates on Gordon's annual Field Day, when students engage in friendly competition and festivities.

BOOK FAIR

This is truly an enriching place. You can feel it the moment you step in the door. It is not just a school, but a community where teachers, staff and parents stop each other in the halls to talk and share pictures, where children are treated with incredible warmth and respect and where smiles and support are abundant.
— Carol Baum, parent of Rebecca '13 and Caleb '16

The GCA Book Fair has celebrated literature for more than fifty years. This major undertaking is organized by volunteers in cooperation with library faculty. In recent years, renowned authors have visited the school to engage students in discussions of writing, illustration and publishing through the Karla Harry Visiting Author Fund, which was founded in 2006 by Almon and Suzanne Hall and their children Stephen '06 and Sara '07, to honor a beloved Gordon librarian.

GORDON SCHOOL

CARNIVAL

The Gordon Community Association delights students and families with the annual GCA Carnival, organized and operated by volunteers who bring their own flavor to the event each year.

Meet Me at the Midway

From the April 21, 1961 edition of *The Providence Journal*.

"Come, come, come to the fair" is the current theme song of the group of mothers who are preparing for the Gordon School's Country Fair.

There will be a midway, pony rides and a plant sale. Homemade baked goods will be on sale in the kitchen cupboard. The cracker barrel and country cheese will be in evidence as well as old-fashioned penny candy.

Preparations for the fair have been underway for months and sale items designed and executed by the mothers are imaginative, gay and useful. There are the traditional smocks and aprons in fanciful color combinations and designs, but most amusing are the items originated by the makers.

Patio candle holders made from juice cans have the look of Mexican tinware and huge hurricane lanterns started out as king-size food containers.

Community

GRANDFRIENDS' DAY

Every year on Grandfriends' Day, Gordon hosts grandparents, parents, relatives and friends of students who spend the day side by side with their special student sharing in their daily school activities.

COMMENCEMENT... A NEW BEGINNING

Commencement is a time for celebration and reflection, a time for moving on and looking back. As students go forward into the next chapter of their education, they do so with unparalleled support from the administration and faculty.

Class of 1926, boys

Class of 1918

Bon Voyage

We are leaving the quiet scenes of childhood; leaving the secluded cove where we have spent our days of happy youth, weathered our own miniature storms, borne up under our childish griefs, and now we are about to go out into the wild, restless expanse of open sea – life. In our sheltered cove we have had careful training. We know which is right and which is wrong and the best course to follow. We also have a secure foundation in which to sail – gathered and hoarded during all these years – a thing that can be increased as time goes on. We are on life's threshold, about to enter into the busy, restless scene we have glimpsed through curtained windows, about to take the clay of life and mold what we will. Best of luck, friends, on the tumultuous sea of life, may we succeed! Bon voyage!

By Peggy Bowen Munsterberg '36, in the 1936 edition of *The Gordonian*.

Class of 1917

Community

I would encourage each of you to take these gifts from Gordon: gifts of wonder and of service; the gift of knowledge and awareness of others; and the gift of wisdom from friends and teachers. Take these gifts to the world: to see, to understand and to be generous.

– Lydia Barlow Faiia '95

Class of 1928, girls

Class of 1943

Class of 1954

Class of 1970

GORDON SCHOOL

(Top right) Faculty members Susan Ginn, Lynn Bowman and Emily Anderson observe Commencement. (Bottom right) Ethan Ruby '89 delivers the Commencement speech in 2007.

Mr. Wales and teachers: you must promise that Gordon keeps teaching all the lessons that the thirty-eight of us have learned so well. Keep bringing in large and lively classes. Let them figure out how they can make a better world. And whatever you do, every spring, take the oldest of them on a Civil Rights trip to the South.

– Dave Hendrie '02, at 2002 Commencement ceremony

Community

The Gordon Experience

We sit here today with heavy hearts knowing Gordon's walls can no longer hold us. We are ready to move on, but sad to go. Graduation day: the day we venture forth from Gordon's protective hug and embark on new experiences.

To an outsider Gordon looks like a rather small school, with a lot of funny pointed roofs. But ask any of us and we will tell you that Gordon is more than an education. When you leave Gordon, you haven't just had an education, you've had an experience that cannot be found anywhere else.

It is an experience of working with friends and having teachers who strive to make sure each individual is in a comfortable learning environment. It is an experience of being allowed to experiment with new things without fear of being set back or embarrassed by failure. It is an experience where you are able to maintain a close relationship with a teacher that you had when you were eight years old and forge a great relationship with a teacher you have when you are thirteen.

It is an experience consisting of nothing less than excellence.

Gregory Katzen '99, from his Commencement speech

Andrew Bower '06 performs the bagpipes at Commencement.

Those going out from Gordon are taking something of it with you, and leaving of themselves here; keep these two somethings alive; come back to the school often.

– Margaret Fulton Coe, Headmistress from 1936-37

GORDON SCHOOL

Qualities of Character

These reflections from valedictorian Isabel Doolittle Wall '33 appeared in the May/June 1933 edition *of The Gordonian.*

To me, graduating is like turning one of the corners in the road. Most of us have been here since the early grades, and have followed the path of disappointment and happiness right through to this class. We have gained knowledge here, much of which will remain with us when we are older, but along the road we have learned other things of even greater importance: we have learned courage, sincerity and truthfulness; those qualities of character will influence the sort of people we are to be.

Community

Karla Harry was a Librarian and Middle School advisor at Gordon from 1999 until her death in 2006. During her last year of life, she served as Interim Director of the Middle School. She gave this advice to the Class of 2006:

Accept difference	Seek wisdom
Value truth	Be kind
Dream	Give freely
Create beauty	Imagine more
Nurture hope	Master something
Show courage	Choose peace
Touch hearts	Express thanks
Trust your instincts	Listen without prejudice
Plant trees	Strive for excellence
Make a difference	Be tolerant
Do something remarkable	Laugh often
Forgive others	Win graciously
Go confidently	Choose with no regret
Learn something everyday	Dwell in possibility
Be grateful	Listen to your heart
Dare to be remarkable	Anything is possible
Trust yourself	Be true to yourself
Be flexible	Find your passion
Question your assumptions	

Appendix

Chairs of the Board of Trustees of the Gordon School
(from 1929, upon the incorporation of the Gordon School, to 2010)

Dr. Arthur Ruggles (1929-1934)
Arthur Livingston Kelly (1934-47)
H. Cushman Anthony (1947-48)
Early Bradley (1948-49)
Bradford Wooley (1949-1951)
William Smith (1951-1954)
Rudy Lowe (1954-1956)
Benjamin A. Smith (1956-1958)
James H. Barnett (1958-1960)
Otto Hoffer (1960-1962)
Martha Livingston, '36 (1963-64)
Dr. Eugene M. Nelson (1964-1967)
James K. Sunshine (1967-69)
Douglas B. Rhodes (1969-1971)
Gilbert Mason (1971-1972)
Lawrence S. Gates (1972-1973)
Bruce Ruttenberg (1973-1976)
Robert H. Goff, Jr. (1976-1978)
George Kilborn (1978-1981)
Austin C. Smith (1981-1983)
Malcolm Chace '48 (1983-84)
Eszter Chase (1984-1986)
Howard M. Kilguss (1986-1988)
Leland Clabots (1989-1990)
Fred J. Franklin (1988-1991)
Jonathan M. Nelson '70 (1991-1994)
Sally E. Lapides (1994-1998)
Barbara H. Hendrie (1998-2001)
Heidi Janes (2001-2004)
Jonathan F. Stone (2004-2007)
Cheryl Nathanson (2007-2010)

Trustees who served ten years or more on the Board as of 2010

Helen West Cooke
John S. Chafee
Olive M. Kelley
Helen Metcalf Danforth
William H. Edwards
Caroline G. Huntoon
Arthur Livingston Kelley
Louise K. Safe
Adelaide B. Viall
Mrs. Edward S. Spicer
Florence L. Robinson
Edward G. Lund
Margaret "Poggy" Langdon
Mrs. Robert H. I. Goddard
Martha Livingston '36
James H. Barnett
Ralph J. Rotkin
James K. Sunshine
Otto Hoffer
Gilbert Mason
Robert H. Goff, Jr.
Laurance Miller
Dr. Eugene M. Nelson
Sally M. Appleton
Darcey Hall-Hale
Jonathan M. Nelson '70
Herb Kaplan
Sally E. Lapides
Thomas C. Keeney
Douglas S. Storrs
Johnnie Chace
Heidi Janes
Jonathan F. Stone
Marcia Hoffer '63
Sara Shea McConnell
Barbara H. Hendrie
Bob Fine '68

Gordon Endowed Funds
Through 2010

Scholarship and Diversity Support

Albanese Fund (1973)
Dr. Eugene M. Nelson Scholarship Fund (1984/1988)
Anna Lolli Memorial Fund (1989)
Gordon Community Association Financial Aid Fund (1991)
Class of 1992 Scholarship Fund
The Ellie and Alfred Fine Scholarship Fund (1992)
The Gordon School Diversity Fund (1992)
The Otto and Elsa Hoffer Financial Aid Fund (1999)
Scholarship Fund for Diversity (Cooks & Books/Hands Around the Table)
The Gordon Scholarship Fund (2001)
Class of 2004 and Barbara Bejoian Financial Aid Fund
Margaret "Poggy" Langdon Financial Aid Fund (2004)
Class of 2006 After School Programs Financial Aid Fund
The David S. Stone Memorial Fund for Financial Aid (2007)
Class of 2009 Financial Aid Fund
Class of 2010 Centennial Financial Aid Fund

Arts Support

Peter Kaplan Memorial Fund (1977)
Ellen D. Grober Memorial Fund (1990)
The Britt Nelson Fund (1996)
The Jonathan D. Arms Fund for Music Education (2009)

Operating Support
The Nicholson Family Fund (1933)
Capital Fund (1985)
Pauline Metcalf Fund (1985)
The Gordon Fund (1992)
The Gordon Community Fund (2008)
The Mary Ann Lippitt '32 Memorial Fund

Facilities Support
The GCA Science Lab Fund (2003)
The Engle Family Athletic Field Fund (2006)

Academic Program Support
The Bready-Lapides Eighth Grade Educational Trip Fund (2003)
Class of 2003 Museum Admissions Fund
The Jeremy, Gregory and Zoe Katzen Science Fund (2003)
The CJ Buckley Fund for Experiential Learning (2005)
Karla Harry Visiting Author Fund (2006)
Class of 2007 Karla Harry Middle School Literature Fund
Class of 2008 Environmental Studies Fund

Professional Development Support
Faculty Training Fund (1984)
Tom Fulton Staff Development Fund (1985)
The Larry Miller Travel Grant (1996)
The Stephen and Sara Hall Science and Math Curriculum Fund (2004)
Class of 2005 Math Curriculum and Professional Development Fund
The Gilbane Family Professional Development Fund (2007)
The Darcey Hall Fund for Professional Advancement

Faculty and Staff Members, 1910 – 2010
(Although compiled from the best available sources, the following list, regrettably, may be incomplete. The dates here correspond to the earliest mentions of the individual in the school's records. If you have information which can help us refine this list, please contact the school.)

Abbatomarco, Patricia (1972)
Abraham, Lauren S. (1987)
Adams, Raymond H., Jr. (1972)
Adams, Sarah G. (1991)
Ahern, Heather (2001)
Alam, Chrys (1986)
Albanese, Melody Ann (1976)
Alexander, Ruth C. (1946)
Allen, Elizabeth F. (1979)
Allen, Kelly A. '01 (2004)
Allen, Rita V. (1996)
Allen, Virginia A. (1996)
Allingham, Caroline P. (1949)
Almeida, Joseph (1999)
Anderson, Emily C. (1998)
Anderson, Philip A. (1990)
Anderson, Inez
Anderson, Joy (1975)
Anderson, Joyce
Anderson, K. Brooke (1934)
Anderson, Philip A.(1990)
Andrew, Thomas S. (1957)
Anthony, Doris (1944)
Anthony, Mary Jane (1944)
Antonelli, Paula M. (1982)
Anzeveno, Kathleen (1985)
Arbuckle, Priscilla
Arcand, Lynne M. (1993)
Arellana, Ruth K. (2003)
Arias, Cendhi (2007)
Arnold, Charles H. (1927)
Arnold, Elizabeth (1943)
Arnold, Genevieve B. (1931)
Artenstein, Debra (2003)
Avizinis, Paul (1978)
Bachelder, Carolotta (1937)
Bacher, Ian C. (1999)
Baird, Aminda S. (1984)
Baker, Christopher R. (1999)

Baker, Martha (1993)
Bakst, Elizabeth F. (1985)
Bancroft, Louise (1940)
Barboza, Alan C. (1983)
Barrett, Andrew W. (2004)
Barsom-Morcos, Norma (2003)
Basler, Harold P. (2004)
Bastos, Jesse (1999)
Baughan, Beverly B. (1980)
Beaudoin, Wilfred R. (1981)
Beaulieu, John R. (1976)
Becker, Jennifer M. (2007)
Belcher, Carlton (1964)
Belcher, Pat (2007)
Beliveau, Carol J. (1981)
Bennett, Leonora B. (1911)
Berardi, Molly C. (1994)
Berkson, Laura (1994)
Berlinksy-Schine, Adam (1998)
Bicki, Lori Giuttari (1998)
Bidwell, Frances G. (1960)
Bigelow, Lois Armstrong (1932)
Bishop, Carl W., Jr. (1981)
Blackman, Sue (1996)
Blackmer, Clare E. (1998)
Blais, Anita (1979)
Blake, Mrs. Charles
Blum, Julia H. (2010)
Boehmke, David (1996)
Bonaccorsi, Deborah
Bonjour, Jeanne C. (1937)
Bonnier, Elisabeth (1994)
Bordman, Margot (1987)
Boswell, Rebecca (2009)
Bottella, Michael J. (1982)
Boudreau, Mr. (1979)
Bowman, Lynn W. (1999)
Boyd, Louise (1959)
Boynton, Rachel C. (1924)

Appendix

Brackett, Catherine (1932)
Bradley, Lee (1951)
Brasil, Mary (1979)
Brathwaite, Collette (1997)
Breed, Mildred C. (1958)
Bresler, Michael (1978)
Bressler, Angelin (1934)
Bride, Melissa B. (2006)
Bride, Jim (1964)
Brigida, Raymond V. (1983)
Brock, Gladys (1936)
Brooke, Miss (1925)
Brown, Dana (2005)
Brown, James P., III (1998)
Brown, Julia (1981)
Brownell, Eleanor (1957)
Bryan, Janet (1943)
Budde, Patricia (1986)
Bugbee, Elizabeth (1940)
Buonanno, Gloria (1947)
Burbank, Louise L. (1996)
Burgess, Dr. Alex M. (1932)
Burlock, Margaret (1954)
Burnham, Anna L. '02 (2008)
Burnham, Janet W. (1992)
Burnham, Rachel J. '97 (2006)
Burns, Mrs. (1954)
Burnstein, Gabriel A. (2009)
Bush-Brown, Mary L. '64 (1975)
Butler, Lisa M. (2009)
Butterfield, Lionel
Buzzi, Hazel (1997)
Calzell, Laura K. (1932)
Camacho, Roseanne V. (1971)
Camet, Patricia (1987)
Campbell, Mary (1932)
Campbell, Mrs. D. Stuart (1940)
Canestrari, Nancy (1985)
Canson, Marian A. (1947)
Cardin, Denise (1978)
Carey, Sarah (1995)
Carichner, Roberta (1967)
Carlson, Elizabeth (1972)

Carman, Melissa J. (2009)
Carneal, Ann Barron (1998)
Carrigan, Joy J. (1978)
Carson, Gregory T. (1999)
Casale, Mary M. (1980)
Cate, Helen (1919)
Cellura, A. Raymond (1972)
Cerjanec, Joan (1993)
Chadwick, Lori (2002)
Champlin, Virginia (1940)
Chase, Geraldine (1937)
Chatellier, Margaret (1996)
Chen, Alice (1972)
Childs, Edith (1924)
Christensen, Eric (2001)
Cicatiello, Thomas J. (1997)
Cicerone, Jolie (2008)
Clark, Margaret
Clark, Sylvia (1932)
Clasper-Torch, Cathy (1990)
Clements, Rosalie B. (1951)
Clemmens, Susan (1984)
Clevenger, Ashley C. (2006)
Coates, Carter R. (1973)
Coates, Leona (1918)
Coe, Margaret F. (1935)
Cohen, Amy L. (1991)
Cohen, Andrew D. (1972)
Colgan, Ann (1955)
Collazo, Carmen D. (2009)
Collett, Alison B. (1968)
Collins, Donald F. (1978)
Collins, Eric P. (2008)
Collins, Mrs. (1920)
Collison, G. Chandler (1993)
Colt, Rosemary P. (2002)
Colwell, Howard T. (1982)
Colyer, C. Carlton (1984)
Comer, Courtney (1979)
Comery, Jean J. (1978)
Cone, Virginia (1968)
Connor, Shanon L. (2008)
Conti, Gino E. (1957)

Coolidge, Mrs. Arlan B. (1934)
Cook, Margery (1940)
Cooke, Dr. Helen West (1910)
Cooke, Elizabeth Cohoe '19 (1930)
Cooper, Dr. Shawn (1976)
Cooper, Ilene
Cooper, Mrs. W. Stewart (1958)
Copp, Gladys (1934)
Cordner, Don (1990)
Cormack, Maribelle (1931)
Cornell, Suzanne (1963)
Costa, Anthony A., Jr. (1981)
Costa, Daniel R. (1957)
Costa, Daniel R., Jr. (1973)
Costa, Isabel
Costa, Mario (2010)
Costa, Mrs. Robert
Couchon, Nancy H. (1972)
Covert, Christopher W. (1987)
Covell, Clarke
Craib, Jessica (2004)
Cram, Mary Lyn (1972)
Crout, Carol C. (1990)
Cruise, Gerald J. (1974)
Cubbage, Mary Lou (1978)
Cucchi, Julie M. (2000)
Cuellar, Silvia (1989)
Cummings, Mr. (1919)
Cusack, Debra J. (1998)
Czepiel, Evelyn E. (1967)
Daily, Roberta A. (1983)
Dalzelle, Laura K. (1932)
Dance, Judith (1990)
Dantzler, Eleanor (1934)
Darcy, Dr. Carol R. (1989)
Davenport, Mary (1968)
Davis, Mark M. (1977)
Davis, Noah '97 (1998)
Davis, Mrs. Earnest, Jr.
Day, Mr. (1925)
Day, Tyler (1951)
Dean, Marsha E. (1972)
DeAngelo, Michael J. (1989)

GORDON SCHOOL

Deason, Elizabeth (1974)
De Barros, Napoleao J. (1989)
DeBlois, James (2000)
Decker, Diane C. (2002)
DeCosta, Mary
Deisroth, Susan (1959)
Delabarre, Barbara (1932)
De Martinez, Mary Therese (2006)
DeMeo, Linda L. (1975)
Denny-Brown, Jack (1977)
Denton, Joya (1984)
dePagter, Maureen (1978)
DeSilva, C. Ivor (1968)
DeSilva, Maureen (1968)
DeStefano, Courtney S. '01 (2007)
DeStefano, Doris (1982)
Dias, Marjorie F. (1999)
Dickey, Miss (1925)
Dimmitt, Mrs. Frank W. (1934)
Dineen, Vanessa K. (1999)
Doben, Margaret (1998)
Dodge, Dorothea (1943)
Don, Mary Ellen (1985)
Donahue, Kerrie F. (2002)
Doppke, P.J. '92 (2005)
Dorsey, F. Blinn (2000)
Downing, Eldon R. (1963)
Downing, Antoinette F. (1940)
Doyle, Cynthia T. (1982)
Driscoll, James R. (1956)
Drummond, Carlton C. (1978)
Duckworth, Phyllis (1949)
Dudzik, Dina (1997)
Duffy, Stephen (1993)
Dugdale, Dorothy M. (1971)
Dulin, Barbara (1973)
Dumas, Suzanne M. (2006)
Dummer, Lisa (1999)
Dumville, Toni (1991)
Dunbar, Marjorie (1943)
Durfee, Steven E. (1989)
Durst, Clare (1973)
Dussault, Susan (1979)
Dutt, Joan (1991)

Dutton, Carolyn-Yvonne (1955)
Dyer, Mrs. Nathaniel B.
Dykhuizen, Suzanne M. (1976)
Earle, Daniel (1932)
Edson, Virginia C. (1947)
Elder, Cynthia A. (2009)
Ellison, Dorie F. (1996)
Emmet, Patricia (1985)
Engelmann, Mrs. Albert C.
Engstrom, Margaret (1998)
Engle, Sarah E. '03 (2008)
Estey, James R. (1962)
Estroff, Samara (2003)
Everett, Anne (1981)
Fabian, Barbara F. (1945)
Fachon, Evangeline M. (1931)
Fahey, Richard (1997)
Falvey, Sandra (1973)
Fanti, Cheryl (1996)
Farley, Paula M. (2006)
Faulise, Lise Gerard (1998)
Faulkner, Mrs. George (1936)
Fazzano, Joanne R. (1989)
Feeley, Kristen (1995)
Feit, Jackie B. (1999)
Feit, Joshua D. (1999)
Feldman, Barbara (1985)
Ferrante, Mrs. Bernard
Field, Claudette (1985)
Finks, Harry (1999)
Fisher, Kathryn (2001)
Fleischner, Ellen (1989)
Fogle-Donmoyer, Amanda H. '95 (2004)
Foley, Jennifer (2001)
Forsten, Charlene (1979)
Forsten, Robert (1979)
Foulke, Kathleen (1993)
Fourgous, Renee (1931)
Fox, Alan
Fox, Suzanne K.F. (2007)
Fraser, Maybury Viall (1950)
Frattaruolo, John (1981)
Fraza, Kristen N. (1994)
Freytag, Katy (2003)

Fritzmeier, William B. (1975)
Fulford, Merilyn (1940)
Fuller, Elizabeth H. (1931)
Fulton, Thomas J. (1983)
Gage, Lauren (2007)
Gamwell, Leona D. (1965)
Gangi, Alyson (2001)
Garcia, Carmen Y. (2005)
Garland, Carroll S. (1981)
Garth, Carolyn (2004)
Gaudet, Derek (1996)
Gaulin, Estelle P. (1966)
Gebhard, Elizabeth (1976)
Geiger, Eleanor (1972)
Genereux, Joan (1993)
Gerdts, George (1993)
Gigone, Otto (1959)
Gill, Harry (1956)
Gilles, Mrs. Frank
Gilley, Ellen (1990)
Gillis, Carolyn
Gilson, Anne B. (1981)
Ginn, Susan M. (2005)
Gladding, Louise R. (1932)
Glancy, Michael M. '94 (1998)
Glancy, Robin P. '97 (1999)
Glancy, Robin S. (1977)
Glinick, Emily B. '98 (1999)
Goddard, Margaret (1937)
Godfrey, Mrs. Richard D. (1961)
Goldberg, Sandra (1982)
Goldberg, Shira R. (1989)
Gomez, Tatiana M. (2008)
Goodman, Celia E. (1913)
Graham, Franklin (1959)
Grann, David (1990)
Granoff, Rosaline (2001)
Grant, Mrs. Hollis E.
Green, David E. (1982)
Greenburg, Gary (1980)
Greenough, Dorothy (1934)
Griffin, Frances (1980)
Griffin, Geoff (2002)
Griffin, Katherine F. (1931)

Griffith, Lisa S. (2003)
Gross, Mrs. Moulton (1936)
Groves, Jeffrey J. (1988)
Guedes, Margarita (2001)
Guilbault, Katherine P. (1998)
Gulick, Charlotte (1937)
Haas, A. Frederick, Jr. (1967)
Hackett, Jill (1997)
Hagan, Natalie A. (1989)
Hagan, Yoshimi (1993)
Haggart, Marcia (1966)
Hagquist, Mrs. Carl (1936)
Hall, Ashley L. (2007)
Hall, Dorothy H. (1985)
Halliwell, Ann (1972)
Ham, Annette Mason (1919)
Ham, Minna (2002)
Hamer, Sean M. (2007)
Hammel, Sandra K. (2002)
Hammer, Mary P. (1936)
Hanley, Christine (1993)
Hansee, Jeanette (1975)
Harders, Paul (1973)
Harding, Ellen (1968)
Harradine, Sylvia (1973)
Harrington, Charles H. (1946)
Harry, Karla (1999)
Hassell, Olga L. (1922)
Hazard, Mary (1950)
Healy, Jacqueline (1968)
Hemenway, Sarah (1997)
Henry, Janet (1941)
Herdrich, Faythe (1984)
Hershey, Eleanor Weber (1959)
Hess, Mrs. Hans Peter (1965)
Heymann, Maryjane '65 (1984)
Higgens, Mrs. John Stuart (1934)
Hill, Jean (1997)
Hincks, Sarah (1936)
Hirschland, Roger B. (1971)
Hoag, Brian (1990)
Hodar, Nancy (1986)
Hodgkins, Mary Ann (1958)
Hodgman, Gail (1931)

Hoffer, David (1994)
Holmes, Margaret R.N. (1983)
Holt, Dorothy (1932)
Hopkins, Barbara G. (1937)
Horr, George
Howard, Gladys (1989)
Howard, Robert T. (1991)
Howe, Meredith (1972)
Hoyt, Ellie (1957)
Hoyt, Mrs. Edwin
Hoyt, Mrs. Fred
Hubbard, Susan (1998)
Hulme, Miss (1972)
Hummel, Mildred T. (1931)
Humphrey, Catherine (1968)
Hunt, Elizabeth (1985)
Hunter, David (1994)
Hutchinson, Cynthia (1937)
Iacono, Janice (1990)
Ida, Mrs. Philip
Imondi, Pompea (2000)
Isidoro, Carlos (1982)
Izman, Paula (1972)
Jackson, Catherine (1973)
Jackson, Robert K. (1972)
Jackson, Mrs. F. Ellis (1911)
Jamieson, Edward B. (1957)
Janis, Jane B. (1958)
Jenness, Rebecca (1999)
Jennings, Patricia A. (1982)
Jobe, Steven L. (1985)
Johnson, Bradford C. (1980)
Johnson, Bri (1997)
Johnson, Carol (1983)
Johnson, Denise L. (1998)
Johnson, Frances H. (1932)
Johnson, Louise (1997)
Johnson, Stephen (1984)
Johnson-Harris, Amy (1980)
Johnston, Barbara L. (1984)
Johnston, Mrs. Thomas J. (1950)
Jones, Allison R. (2005)
Jones, Cornelia (1987)
Jungels, Rachel (1990)

Jutras, Veronica R. (2007)
Kallem, Gillis (1993)
Kanchanagom, Patra (2000)
Kantarovsky, Masha (1997)
Karas, Alexandra N. (2009)
Karahalis, Julia (1996)
Karpf, Daniel (2006)
Kelly, Maureen D. (1980)
Kelly, Tricia A. (2008)
Ketner, Jacqueline (1985)
Kimball, Miriam S. (1986)
King, Helen (1994)
King, Joanne (2006)
Kingman, Miss (1954)
Kippax, Glenn T. (1949)
Kiskhovich, Elena (1998)
Kline, Stephanie (1998)
Kline, Valerie (1998)
Knapp, Jane W. (1938)
Knott, Dorothy (1928)
Knowles, Ethel Elizabeth (1934)
Koelb, Janice M. (1959)
Kolton, Brooke L. (1973)
Kranz, Clara P. (1939)
Krause, Carol (1973)
Kravitz, Eric G. (1997)
Kravitz, Samantha (2003)
Kronquist, Katherine B. (1943)
Kruk, Kay (2002)
Lachman, Elsie Philips (1959)
Langdon, Frances (1940)
Langdon, Margaret "Poggy" (1939)
Lanyi, Susan (1949)
LaPane, Leo H. (1977)
Laporte, Paul M. (1940)
LaRocque, Joyce (1981)
Lasiewski, Doreen (1981)
Lawall, Lina Ann (1972)
Lawrence, Laura McNamara (1993)
Lazarus, Lisa (1996)
Leach, Mrs. Douglas
Leach, Sarah (1972)
Lee, Willie (2000)
Leventhal, Phyllis (1998)

Levin, Mrs. Gerald (1959)
Lial, Frank
Lind, Andrew H. (2005)
Locke, Frederic W. (1956)
Lombardi, Jim (1948)
Look, Arnold
Lougee, Grace H. (1949)
Lovejoy, Elizabeth B. (1947)
Lowe, Miss (1926)
Lund, Edward G. (1939)
Lydon, Louise (1993)
MacArthur, Harvey H. (1967)
MacGregor, Stuart (1999)
Machado, Camely (2007)
Machado, Jose G. (2000)
Mackenzie, Mrs. Gavin (1964)
MacNamee, Peter (1976)
MacPherson, Carol (1969)
Mahoney, Kevin (1990)
Mahoney, Thomas R. (1959)
Manchester, Myra L. (1921)
Mann, Debra (2001)
Manter, Miss (1927)
Margulies, Mrs. S. Jerry
Marinaccio, Frank (1989)
Marshall, Rona (2000)
Martell, Lorraine, R.N. (1994)
Martin, Laura J. (1999)
Martindale, Frances (1995)
Martinez, Paola A. (2005)
Martinez, Ruben Jose (2005)
Mason, Nancy (1947)
Mason, R. Brenda (1949)
Master, Patricia (1971)
McAdam, Robert (2002)
McCafferty, James J. (1984)
McCalmont, Susan (1990)
McCarthy, Carol (1960)
McCarthy, Mrs. Eugene F.
McCormick, Kate (2002)
McConnell, Miss (1914)
McDowell, Barbara (1993)
McElroy, Barbara (2001)
McGough, Kathy (2002)

McIntire, Catherine (1941)
McIntyre, Mrs. George F.
McIntyre, Mrs. Ronald
McKenna, Florence (1978)
McLaughlin, Robert C. (1959)
Meader, Margaret Gammell (1918)
Meardon, J. Arnold (1966)
Medeiros, Marjorie (1972)
Mello, Manuel M. (1990)
Mercer, Mrs. (1957)
Mercer, Paul L. (1962)
Mercurio, Kate (2006)
Merserau, Mrs. Howard
Metzger, Miss (1921)
Meyer-Eisendrath, Jessie (2001)
Meyers, Barbara (1940)
Meyers, Judith (1973)
Michaud, Eleanor (2005)
Micoleau, Tyler (1942)
Milkowski, George (1997)
Miller, Helen (1968)
Miller, Laurance P. (1960)
Miller, Marion (1932)
Miller, Thomas G. (1993)
Miner, Katherine (1943)
Miranda, Lisa A. (1989)
Mongeon, Kimberly S. (2001)
Monti, Christopher (2007)
Moore, Erin (2000)
Moore, Nancy J. (1993)
Moore, Steven (1989)
Morgan, Barbara (1972)
Morrow, Peggy (1957)
Morse, Felicity (1957)
Morse, Peter (1990)
Moses, Mrs. John G. (1951)
Motta, Neville N. '75 (2003)
Moulton, Barbara S. (1943)
Mulick, Nancy E.W. (1981)
Mullen, Sarah K. (2008)
Mullin, Linda (1982)
Munslow, Stan (1997)
Murray, Bruce
Myers, Susan (1972)

Myette, Margaret E. (1997)
Nash, Ann (1958)
Nelson, Harold J. (1968)
Nelson, Jane (1968)
Neves, Anthony (1981)
Neville, Margaret R. (1973)
Newbold, Timothy J. (2006)
Nichols, Alice M. (1978)
Nichols, Dr. Ira (1932)
Nichols, Mrs. Roger B. (1950)
Nicholson, Mary Elizabeth (1943)
Nicodemus, Emily (1993)
Nilson, Micheline
Noelte, Barbara
Noonan, Herbert I. (1960)
Nowell, Mrs. John
O'Connor, Lisa (1993)
Odean, Kathleen F. (2005)
O'Donnell, Kimberly M. (1994)
O'Hara, Joan P. (1988)
Olchowski, Bonnie M. (1989)
Olean, Bruce (1972)
O'Mahoney, Leah (1982)
O'Neill, Alice D. (1999)
O'Neill, Clare (1999)
O'Neill, Mrs. (1949)
Oster, Bernard D. (1962)
Oster, Daphne (1973)
Oster, Michael (1997)
Owen, Mrs. Allen F. (1962)
Padillia, Piper (1986)
Page, George C. (1990)
Palmieri, Dana (1990)
Pannell, Elizabeth J. (2008)
Parikh, Sarika (2001)
Parisi, Dorothy
Parker, Mrs. Mason (1950)
Parmentier, Mlle. (1917)
Parsons, Julie (2003)
Patterson, Nancy (1978)
Paulson, Marion L. (1957)
Pawlowski, Tess (1998)
Peck, Marilyn (1941)
Pedersen, Lynne P. (1976)

Peebles, Scott (2001)
Pepin, Elias (1939)
Pereira, Elaine
Perry, David D. (1978)
Perry, Helen (1940)
Petruzzi, Selena K. (2008)
Pezzulli, Suzanne M. (2007)
Phinney, Joanna (1973)
Pierce, Donna (1983)
Pieri, Maryanne D. (1995)
Pieri, Paul (1997)
Pina, Shai R. (2003)
Pinkham, David S. (1993)
Podmore, Amy (1983)
Polite, Eric, II (2002)
Poole, Denise (1989)
Porter, Carol (1995)
Porter, Gail N. (2000)
Powell, Matthew (1999)
Prario, Richard T. (2001)
Presby, Miss (1916)
Previdi, Laura (1998)
Price, Adam (2001)
Pronga, Cheyenne (2003)
Provonsil, Kathryn M. (1989)
Pullitzer, Mrs. (1955)
Punchak, Amy (2001)
"Queenie" (1948)
Quevedo, Mercedes H. (1961)
Quill, Heidi M. (1975)
Radway, Mrs. Robert W.
Raff, Laura (1979)
Ramos, Manuel G. (1980)
Ramsdell, Frances H. (1932)
Ramsdell, Mrs. Donald A. (1934)
Randolph, Mrs. John (1959)
Ranger, Miss (1921)
Reed, Betsy (1968)
Reed, Bette (1954)
Reed, Mrs. Thomas L. (1951)
Reeves, Diana O. (1991)
Rehm, Barbara (1974)
Reid, Peter
Reid, Roslyn (1963)

Rempis, Alexandros C. (2008)
Reynolds, Constance H. (1949)
Rhee, Mrs. Kendall
Rhodes, Christine (2001)
Rice, Jane (1972)
Rice, Winifred (1913)
Richard, Ida (1949)
Richardson, Marian L. (1936)
Ridley, Kimberly T. (2008)
Riege, Virginia (1978)
Riegel, Amanda G. (2009)
Rinn, Inez (1932)
Roberts, Jane
Robertson, Heidi (1972)
Robinson, Florence L. (1944)
Robinson, Margaret (1982)
Rockwell, Miss (1917)
Rollins, Jennifer Jean "Ife" (2003)
Romanzi, Milly (2008)
Rosenbaum, Judith (1977)
Roseberg, Alan (1977)
Roterman, Mimi (2008)
Rouslin, Mrs. (1957)
Rubovits, Pamela (1993)
Ruggles, Dr. Arthur H. (1934)
Rusk, Katherine Gaul (1931)
Russo, Vinnie (1994)
Ruth, Dr. Eugene D., Jr. (1980)
Saltonstall, Kerry (1995)
Samuel, Afiya A. (2007)
Sandall, Sarah S. (2003)
Sandoli, Felix
Sandow, Dana (1983)
Sangalang, Belle (2009)
Santos, Eugene (1994)
Saunders, Shirley (2000)
Sawin, Moulton (1944)
Schiff, Mrs. Arthur
Schneider, Lucy Ann (1941)
Schwedersky, Mrs. George
Scott, Abigail (2007)
Scott, Barbara J. (1985)
Scott, Sharon (1990)
Seegar, Elizabeth (1932)

Segar, Jane (1972)
Selzer, Aaron (1980)
Sewall, Hilda (1943)
Shabalin, Alexey (1998)
Shah-Hosseini, Mitra (1998)
Share, Mrs. Lawrence J. (1960)
Sharp, Walter (1941)
Shay, Fred
Sherba, Consuelo (1993)
Shippee, Mrs. Harold, Jr. (1964)
Shumway, Diane
Siegel, Tovia A. (1978)
Silva, Joan W. (1976)
Silva, Manuel (1978)
Simister, Lillian L. (1923)
Simmons, Helen (1973)
Simmons, Marian (1977)
Simon, Lindsay A. (2006)
Singelton, Carleton (1950)
Skillings, James A. (1997)
Sluss, Santana (1990)
Smart, Marion
Smith, Aaron (1979)
Smith, Barbara (1984)
Smith, Carroll (1980)
Smith, Dottie (1993)
Smith, Michael H. (1986)
Smith, Miss Gene (1934)
Smith, Prudence (1940)
Smith, Susan H. (1980)
Smith, William (1943)
Snow, Wileen (2007)
Snyder, Mrs. Allen (1943)
Snyder, Stephen (1983)
Soch, Augusta (1928)
Soper, Stephanie (1985)
Soukassian, Miss (1954)
Sousa, Alicia P. (1965)
Souza, Joseph M. (1949)
Spangler, Tina (1999)
Speelman, Deborah (1987)
Spence, Cynthia G. (1997)
Sperduti, Maria (1985)
Sperry, Barbara (1943)

GORDON SCHOOL

Spicer, Barbara (1972)
Sprague, Lloyd F. (1966)
Staebler, Albert (1993)
Staebler, Patricia H. (1974)
Stauffer, Anne
Steitz, Mrs. Robert A. (1965)
Stengel, Robin (1975)
Sterrett, Marianne C. (1989)
Stevens, Anne (1998)
Stewart, Caroline T. (1962)
Stillman, Judith (1998)
Strachan, Barbara (1936)
Streisand, Iveth Z. (2009)
Stringfellow, Mrs. (1914)
Struder, Patricia (1959)
Surette, Thomas Whitney (1932)
Sutton, Thelma (1984)
Swazey, Mrs. (1955)
Sweeney, Anne T. (1984)
Sweikert, Robert (2002)
Swierk, Jamie (2002)
Sylvia, Nancy A. (1980)
Szczepanowska, Anna (2005)
Tally, Mrs. William E. (1966)
Tate, Frances (1981)
Teatrowe, Bruce (1989)
Terr, Lyndia
Terzian, Debra Lynn (1985)
Thompson, Buffi (2000)
Thornley, Dorothy J. (1965)
Thumith, Deborah (1989)
Tillinghast, Grace (1948)
Tolbert, Victoria (2001)
Toothaker, Susanne B. (1998)
Townley, Mary Ross (1963)
Trask, Mary B. (1955)
Traver, Belle H. (1968)
Traver, Sarah (1979)
Tremblay, Esther (1961)
Tripp, Ruth E. (1949)
Troy, George Jr. (1932)
Truscott, Mary (1951)
Tsonas, Nicole (1979)
Tudino, Michael V. (1997)

Tulip, Emma C. (1920)
Tuttle, Lawrence E. (1986)
Tyler, Mrs. (1930)
Tyston, Laura (1972)
Utter, Dr. Henry F. (1932)
Vadeboncoeur, Clare (1997)
Vartian, Kevin S. (2009)
Vaughan, Catherine (1999)
Vaughn, Dana Prescott (1932)
Vaughn, Jeanne-Marie, R.N. (1997)
Vaughn, Miss (1922)
Vaughn, Roger E. (1959)
Viall, Gretchen (1981)
Vinhateiro, June Stone (1984)
Voccio, Frank (1984)
Vogt, Herbert G. (1940)
Voll, Nondas H. (1975)
Vorenberg, Katie (2000)
Wagner, Tanna (2001)
Wales, Ralph L. (1994)
Walker, Veodis G. (1968)
Wallace, Andrew (2001)
Wallace, Nellie F.R. (1931)
Walters, Noelle C. (2005)
Wardwell, Barbara (1932)
Waterman, Paula (1968)
Watson, Joann K. (1971)
Weaver, Miss (1930)
Webb, Joan M. (1978)
Webber, Kathryn M. (1998)
Weeks, Virginia E. (1946)
Wells, Barbara (1975)
Wells, David P. (1977)
Welsh, Siobhan Sheerar (2006)
Wender, Anna M., R.N. (1932)
West, Matthew D. (1997)
Whinery, Sarah W. (1988)
White, Annie '87 (2007)
White, Carolyn R. (1988)
White, Elizabeth "Poo" (1993)
White, Eric J. (2006)
White, Griselda (1966)
White, Kristin
White, Mrs. James (1951)

Whitehead, Phyllis
Whitney, Linda (1982)
Whittan, Mr. (1925)
Widerman, James L. (1972)
Wilbur, Janet (1951)
Wilcox, Lucy F. (1932)
Wilkinson, Virginia (1931)
Wilks, Adam P. (1997)
Williams, Janet (1940)
Willis, Suzanne (1968)
Wilson, Judith M. (1975)
Wilson, Mrs. Earnest M. (1964)
Windham, Carolyn M. (1981)
Winfield, Nancy (1989)
Winn, Ruth T. (1962)
Wise, Miss (1920)
Withrow, George (1960)
Withrow, Kay (1989)
Withrow, Scott (1990)
Wood, Anne K. (1958)
Woodhouse, Barbara (1972)
Woodruff, Helen (1931)
Woodruff, Mrs. Joe (1971)
Woodward, Mrs. Arthur A. (1949)
Wrenn, Harriet C. (1978)
Wright, Elliott (1974)
Wyman, Ethel (1956)
Wynne, Frances M. (2007)
Wynne, Megan (2007)
Young, Ann (1932)
Young, Juliann (1998)
Zakin, Rebecca B. (2009)
Zipin, Beth (1979)
Zoglio, Suzanne
Zurawel, Rosemary (1976)
Zuromski, Alice (1977)